LIVING EVERY
MOMENT RIGHTLY
FOR JESUS

Naphtali Iringe-Koko

Grosvenor House
Publishing Limited

This book is published by
Grosvenor House Publishing Ltd
Link House
140 The Broadway, Tolworth, Surrey, KT6 7HT.
www.grosvenorhousepublishing.co.uk

A CIP record for this book
is available from the British Library

Paperback ISBN 978-1-83975-830-0
Hardback ISBN 978-1-80381-233-5

ABOUT THE AUTHOR

---- ❋ ----

Naphtali Iringe-Koko was born into a Christian family. His father was a local fisherman and the family lived on subsistence fishing. He was educated through the Anglican Mission Schools for his primary and secondary education. He is a chartered accountant (CIMA & ICAN) with a career that spanned a couple of decades with both the private and public sectors (UAC of Nigeria PLC (UACN), NNPC, OPEC, Nigeria LNG Limited (NLNG)).

Naphtali is a member of the Nigerian Environmental Society (NES) and the author of two books. The first is titled *Balancing Commercial Interests with Environmental and Socio-Economic Responsibilities in the Nigerian Oil and Gas Industry*. The second book is titled *Nigeria LNG: A Dream Come True after 35 years of Hope in the Balance*. He has contributed to sharing the environmental message from an accounting and sustainable development perspective.

Naphtali has shared his Christian faith both locally and internationally. He was one of the church leaders at the Vienna International Baptist Church Austria. He has served as a Sunday school and weekly youth Bible studies teacher and he hosted weekly adult Bible studies. He served as the head of church ushers and treasurer. The account of his upbringing in Chapter 22 has further details about the author.

ACKNOWLEDGEMENT

This book was written in the midst of the covid-19 pandemic in my village, as highlighted in my covid-19 experience during the lockdown in Chapter 23. I owe a debt of gratitude to my family for their support and to individuals who inspired me. Most importantly, I thank the Almighty God for providing a calm and peaceful environment in my home, which enabled me to write this book in the midst of the pandemic.

PREFACE

❋

As the table of content demonstrates, I have uncountable reasons for writing this book. What is said here is a drop in the ocean. I had the urge to share my experience of the struggle to serve Jesus through a very challenging upbringing and highly challenging career path in a world without compassion, mercy or justice. Despite all these challenges, I emerged victorious. The gospel of grace touched my life and I owe the Almighty God the duty to share my experiences of how God is good not because I am good but because He is good. Such testimonies do not only serve as encouragement to other believers but also promote the work of the ministry. Christ wants believers to share their experiences on how the Lord is good (Mark 5:19). In Acts 4:19-20, when the leaders of the Jews wanted Peter and John not to share their testimonies about Jesus' miracles, they answered, "We cannot help speaking about what we have seen and heard". Jesus instructs that prayers are to be made in His name. Praying to God through the name of Jesus is effective and powerful when the believer is connected to Jesus through genuine faith in him. Without Christ interceding for us in prayers, God will not listen to our prayers.

I feel a book of this nature will help believers always reflect on their relationship with Jesus, ensuring that they are in union with him. This book has also been written as a reminder to every believer that in whatever vocation you find yourself, remember that you are the messenger. Your life should speak for Jesus. This book was written in the midst of the covid-19 pandemic storm and sharing my experience will make an interesting read for inspiration.

Finally, the writing of this book has not been made possible because of my command of the Bible or self-righteousness or persuasive skills. My confidence in writing this book is from God, who breathed the Bible, and with guidance from the Holy Spirit.

TABLE OF CONTENT

———— ✳ ————

Chapter 1

INTRODUCTION

The Bible is the authoritative guide for all believers. It is the word of spirit and of power, breathed by God and inspired by the Holy Spirit. Living every moment rightly for Jesus is a book specifically written to help believers serve Jesus rightly in whatsoever engagements they find themselves according to what the Bible says and not according to what individuals feel or think. The word of God is the absolute truth and what it says is the absolute truth for all of us. If we abide by the word, we will be serving God according to the spirit-guided way of living. The book will help believers walk in the light. It will help us not to be out of control in walking with Jesus, because he is our focus and our power source. The Bible is our lamp that guides our feet and lights our path, ensuring that our steps are held to his path and our feet do not slip. The book will also help believers avoid self-righteousness and ending up in compromising the word of God. Life is about the journey more than the destination because of the storms, mountains and valleys we need to surmount to become finishers. The word of God is our compass for navigating through all obstacles. God is a jealous God. He does not want any competition for our loyalty (Nahum 1:2; Deut. 32:16). Living every moment rightly for Jesus will help believers put God first in their lives.

This book is also used as a source of sharing my personal experiences in my struggle to serve Jesus and my testimony of how God is good and how the gospel of grace touched my life. Life is not a contest; it is a chance to do the best you can with what you have and according to what the word of God says. Furthermore, this book was written during my covid-19 pandemic isolation and lockdown in my village home in 2020 to early 2021. The few testimonies mentioned in the book are a drop in the ocean of how the gospel of grace touched my life and those around me. A short brief on the covid-19 pandemic storm and my experience during the pandemic are interesting read for inspiration.

More importantly, this book is written as my humble contribution towards promoting the ministry of Jesus and also to thank the God Almighty for his goodness. All support received from the purchase of this book will be channeled towards promoting the work of the focused ministry through the needy areas of society. The Bible passages quoted in this book are from the New International Version (NIV).

The Word of Spirit and of Power

1 John 2:6

Whoever claims to live in him must walk as Jesus did.

Psalm 119:105

Your word is a lamp to my feet and a light to my path.

Psalm 17:4-5

As for the deeds of men – by the words of your lips I have kept myself from the ways of the violent. My steps have held to your paths; my feet have not slipped.

Proverbs 6:22-23

When you walk, they will guide you; when you sleep, they will watch over you; when you awake, they will speak to you. For these commands are a lamp, this teaching is a light, and the corrections of discipline are the way to life.

Isaiah 30:21

Whether you turn to the right or to the left, your ears will hear a voice behind you, saying, "This is the way; walk in it".

John 8:12

When Jesus spoke again to the people, he said, "I am the light of the world. Whoever follows me will never walk in darkness, but will have the light of life".

2 Peter 1:19

And we have the word of the prophets made more certain, and you will do well to pay attention to it, as to a light shining in a dark place, until the day dawns and the morning star rises in your hearts.

2 Timothy 3:16-17

All scripture is God-breathed and is useful for teaching, rebuking, correcting and training in righteousness, so that the man of God may be thoroughly equipped for every good work.

Ephesians 6:11, 17

Put on the full amour of God so that you can take your stand against the devil's schemes. Take the helmet of salvation and the sword of the spirit, which is the word of God.

1 John 2:5

But if anyone obeys his word, God's love is truly made complete in him. This is how we know we are in him.

1 John 2:3-4

We know that we have come to know him if we obey his commands. The man who says, "I know him," but does not do what he commands is a liar, and the truth is not in him.

Chapter 2

THE CROSS AND THE CHURCH

---- ✳ ----

Sacrificial lambs shed their blood on the altar for the sins of Israel, but Jesus Christ shed his blood on the cross for the sins of the world (John 1:29). His death on the cross was a horrifying event through which he died for our sins (Gal. 1:4). Jesus endured the cross, scorning its shame so that we might be reconciled with God by his shed blood (Col. 1:20). God's curse on sin is death. Jesus carried God's curse on sin upon himself in order to free us from that curse (Gal 3:13). Jesus showed the humble nature of his mission and ministry through his obedience to death, even death on the cross (Phil. 2:8). The event of the cross is a model of obedience and love in the Bible.

The cross is Jesus Christ. It reveals the unconditional love of God in offering his one and only son as the sacrificial Lamb to atone for our sins (John 3:16). Jesus fulfilled the requirements of the law on the cross to make us righteous when we put our faith in him. The cross is a symbol of sacrificial love, obedience and selflessness. The church is the body of Christ and should lead in proclaiming the message of the cross as Christ directed. The message of the cross is not negotiable. It is by the cross that believers become triumphant over the powers of darkness (Col. 2:15). This message is essential for a world that is becoming more ungodly and sliding towards materialism. The temptation to water down the message of the cross to attract church membership and patronage must be resisted. Jesus Christ did not water down his message to attract followers. In crusade and evangelism venues, the focus is more on breakthroughs, prosperity, miracles, healing, speaking in tongues, prophecy, and so on, while the message of the cross is either minimised or ignored. These benefits

4

are available to believers, but we must seek first his kingdom and his righteousness, and these things will be given to us as well (Matt. 6:33). In Luke 8:18, Jesus says, "Consider carefully how you listen". 1 Timothy 4:1 tells us that, "The Spirit clearly says that in later times some will abandon the faith and follow deceiving spirits and things taught by demons". In Matthew 7:22-23, Jesus says, "Many will say to me on that day, Lord, Lord, did we not prophesy in your name, and in your name drive out demons and perform many miracles? Then I will tell them plainly, I never knew you. Away from me you evildoers". Galatians 1:8 says, "But even if we or an angel from Heaven should preach a gospel other than the one we preached to you, let him be eternally condemned".

The Message of The Cross

Whenever I gaze at the cross, what I see is sacrificial love, holiness, sinlessness, faithfulness, patience, obedience, righteousness, goodness, selflessness, mercy, justice, perseverance, repentance and forgiveness. These are the components of the message of the cross. In a world that is fast sliding into ungodliness and materialism, the message of the cross should count and should not be compromised for the sake of attracting patronage and membership. Jesus Christ did not compromise his teaching to attract followers. What people hear on the pulpit is what they apply in their spiritual growth and conduct. The message of the cross is what will help people conduct themselves in a manner worthy of the gospel of Christ and make their lives speak for Jesus. By their fruit you will recognise them (Matt. 7:20). The message of the cross and righteousness cannot be exchanged with tithing, offering and donations. In Mathew 23:23, Christ says, "Woe to you, teachers of the law and Pharisees, you hypocrites. You give a tenth of your spices –mint, dill and cumin. But you have neglected the more important matters of the law – justice, mercy and faithfulness. You should have practised the latter, without neglecting the former". The message of the cross is absolutely necessary for a world that is fast sliding into ungodliness and materialism. Accepting Christ is not just about accepting his miracles. You must carry the cross. In the miracle of two fishes in John 6:1-13, Jesus fed 5000 people with two fishes. They accepted his miracle, but they refused to accept what Christ said. All the 5000 went away. Likewise Nicodemus believed in Christ miracles and not his teaching (John 3:1-5).

Sin is at the center of the Bible plan, and is an enemy of God. Christ shed his blood on the cross because of our sins. Sin is still plaguing the world in this present age, and should be central in delivering the message of the cross. Even though sin may be an inconvenience to many, we cannot leave it out of the message of the cross or water it down. To some, sin is the most unpleasant subject to preach, but for true Christians it is the way forward to reducing human wickedness, discrimination, inequality, corruption and ungodly desires. Furthermore, sin stunts growth in Christians. It prevents them from attaining their full potential. When we accept and believe in Jesus, we receive new life. God wants us to be fruitful and demonstrate this new life among those around us. Sin will affect our ability to realise God's purpose for us. How do we make our nations, governments, communities, cities, towns become prosperous, caring, hospitable, peaceful, lovable, and friendly if we do not share the message of the cross? Christians are the light of the world and salt of the earth. Christianity changed the primitive life of Africa, and also led to the end of the slave trade. Jesus tells his disciples to take up the cross and follow him. He did not say it should be once a year, or once a month, but day by day and moment by moment (Luke 9:23). Church-going does not make you a Christian. What makes you a Christian is the fruit you bear. Christians bear fruit outside the four walls of the church, by doing what Christ has asked them to do.

The Truth about Sin

The Bible, starting from Genesis to Revelation, shows that sin is a central issue in the Bible plan. Sin is the fundamental problem that must be solved to enable God's purpose for creation to be completed. The world is not evil. God created the world and blessed it and says it is very good (Gen. 1:31). The problem of the world is that it has been corrupted by human sin. When baptised into Christ Jesus, Christians are counted as dead to sin and are expected to live a new life (Rom. 6:1-4). However the fact that we are dead to sin when we accept Christ Jesus does not mean we are incapable of sinning again. To sin or not depends on the extent of the person's old nature and new nature. Although Christians continue to struggle with sin (Rom. 8:12-13; Gal. 5:16-25), sin should no longer have dominion over them. The Holy Spirit empowers them to fight sin (Gal. 5:16-18). Being descendants of the first man Adam, every person born into the world is a sinner and therefore sins (Rom. 5:12-14). A Christian cannot be sinless. Jesus Christ is the only sinless person who has ever lived (Heb. 9:13-14). A believer (Christian) must be a person whose life is being changed by God through the gospel. He must be a person who repents day by day; a person who never gives up the daily struggle against sin and the devil (1 Tim. 4:16).

1 John 1:9 says, "If we confess our sins, he is faithful and just and will forgive us our sins and purify us from all unrighteousness". Sin affects every aspect of a person's life such as actions, emotions, heart, mind, will, tongue, lips, motives and nature. Genesis 6:5 says, "The LORD saw how great man's wickedness on the Earth had become and that every inclination of the thoughts of his heart was only evil all the time". Apostle Paul in Romans 3:10-18 describes the extent of human sin by saying, "There is no one righteous, not even one; there is no one who understands, no one who seeks God. All have turned away; they have together become worthless; there is no one who does good, not even one. Their throats are open graves; their tongues practice deceit. The poison of vipers is on their lips. Their mouths are full of cursing and bitterness. Their feet are swift to shed blood, ruin and misery mark their ways; and the way of peace they do not know. There is no fear of God before their eyes". Proverbs 6:16-17 says, "There are six things the LORD hates, seven that are detestable to him: haughty eyes, a lying tongue, hands that shed innocent blood, a heart that devises wicked schemes, feet that are quick to rush into evil, a false witness who pours out lies, and a man who stirs up dissension among brothers".

Consequences of Sin

Because of the sin of Adam, the whole creation lived in darkness. Due to his disobedience, all the original cordial relationships with God were broken (Gen. 3:1-24). Mankind became the enemy of God, and came under the curse of God's judgment and became unworthy to stand before God. As a result of sin, God cursed the ground to resist human efforts to cultivate it and made it to grow thorns and thistles (Gen. 3:17-18).

The covenant at Sinai which God made with Israel was predicated on obedience to the law (Exod. 19:5-6). The sacrificial system was the focus of the covenant with Israel which God provided as the means of atoning their sins. The people of Israel repeatedly and persistently broke God's covenant with them. Even at the highest level of prosperity under King David and his son Solomon, sin plagued the people of Israel including its kings. David was involved in adultery and murder (2 Sam. 11:1-27). Solomon had hundreds of foreign wives and concubines who turned his heart from Yahweh to other gods (1 Kings 11:1-8). The consequences of sin resulted in a divided nation which split into two (Israel and Judah), and finally went into exile from the land (Israel in 722 BC, Judah in 586 BC).

In this present time, sin is recognised as the polluter of society and its structures corrupting nations, governments, economic and social structures just to mention but a few. Sin such as corruption and wickedness has made it difficult to attain economic and social progress for all in various parts of the world. Poverty, greed, discrimination, inequality persist due to sin. In addition, sin causes conflict between individuals and harms relationships of all kinds. Sin is the foundation for mistrust, selfishness, jealousy, and greed that infect even the closest relationships.

Sin makes humanity guilty in God's court of law. It makes us become God's enemies and brings us God's righteous wrath. Romans 1:18 says, "The wrath of God is being revealed from Heaven against all the godlessness and wickedness of men who suppress the truth by their wickedness".

The church is the rightful avenue to address the sins of the world in this present age. God has given the church Pastors and teachers, approved workmen and women whom their various ministries are able to assist us to understand and believe and live in response to the word which God has spoken. James 5:19-20 says, "My brothers, if one of you should wander from the truth and someone should bring him back, remember this: whoever turns a sinner from the error of his way will save him from death and cover over a multitude of sins".

Despite the presence of some false teachers and prophets, the church is where believers are equipped for the ministry of Jesus. In Matthew 24:4-5, Christ said, "Watch out that no one deceives you. For many will come in my name claiming, I am the Christ and will deceive many". False prophets and teachers will ultimately receive their punishment (2 Peter 2:1-9). We must trust in the spirit of Christianity so strongly that we will never abandon the faith to those who use it as a camouflage for selfish interest.

In conclusion, the church cannot really make meaningful impact on a society that is fast sliding into ungodliness without strong commitment to sharing the message of the cross. People cannot advance spiritually apart from what they hear on the pulpit. The problem of man is sin. The fall of man is sin. Eternity is most important. The object of our faith is the cross. The cross is Christ. We cannot separate the person of Christ and the cross.

A Short Checklist for the Church

1) Are the churches being used truly for God's purpose?
2) Is evangelism being used truly for God's purpose?
3) Is prophesy being used truly for God's purpose?
4) Jesus drove out those selling animals for sacrifice in the temple because of commercialising it (profiteering).
5) God does not tempt us but allows things to happen to us to change us to his ways.

6) Is preaching the message of the cross becoming an inconvenience because of the concern of losing patronage and membership?

7) Christ did not water-down his message to attract followers.

The Word of Spirit and of Power

Genesis 2:16-17

And the LORD God commanded the man, "You are free to eat from any tree in the garden; but you must not eat from the tree of the knowledge of good and evil, for when you eat of it you will surely die."

Genesis 3:17-18

To Adam he said, "Because you listened to your wife and ate from the tree about which I commanded you, 'You must not eat of it'. Cursed is the ground because of you, through painful toil, you will eat of it all the days of your life. It will produce thorns and thistles for you and you will eat the plants of the field".

Jeremiah 12:4

How long will the land lie parched and the grass in every field be withered? Because those who live in it are wicked, the animals and birds have perished.

Romans 8:22

We know that the whole creation has been groaning as in the pains of childbirth right up to the present time.

Genesis 6:5

The LORD saw how great man's wickedness on the earth had become, and that every inclination of the thoughts of his heart was only evil all the time.

Genesis 8:21

The LORD smelled the pleasing aroma and said in his heart, "Never again will I curse the ground because of man, even though every inclination of his heart is evil from childhood".

10

Jeremiah 17:9

The heart is deceitful above all things and beyond cure. Who can understand it?

Romans 5:12-14

Therefore, just as sin entered the world through one man, and death through sin, and in this way death came to all men, because all sinned, for before the law was given, sin was in the world. But sin is not taken into account when there is no law. Nevertheless, death reigned from the time of Adam to the time of Moses, even over those who did not sin by breaking a command, as did Adam, who was a pattern of the one to come.

Romans 1:18

The wrath of God is being revealed from heaven against all the godlessness and wickedness of men who suppress the truth by their wickedness.

Chapter 3

WHAT DOES GOD'S RIGHTEOUSNESS MEAN TO THE WORLD?

—— ✳ ——

God reigns in righteousness. Righteousness and justice are the foundation of God's throne (Ps. 97:2; Ps. 89:14). God's righteousness is divine righteousness without sin, and completely holy in his actions (John 17:25). His Laws are righteous (Rom. 7:12); God is a righteous judge (2 Tim. 4:8). God reigns over his creation in righteousness. His son, Our Lord Jesus Christ is righteous (1 John 2:1). Jesus Christ is the only sinless person who has ever lived (1 John 3:5). Jesus Christ's righteousness fulfilled God's righteousness which met all human righteous requirements for salvation through faith in Him (2 Peter 1:1). Human righteousness is described in the Bible as filthy rags which would have made our justification and redemption impossible (Isa. 64:6). Therefore God made him who had no sin to be sin for us so that in him we might become the righteousness of God (2 Cor. 5:21). He himself bore our sins in his body on the tree, so that we might die to sins and live for righteousness; by his wounds you have been healed (1 Peter 2:24). There is power in the blood of Jesus because it is through the blood of Jesus that we become the righteousness of God, making our salvation possible when we believe and put our faith in him. The righteousness of God is unattainable by humans. Human righteousness is unacceptable in providing justification and redemption for our sins. Christ righteousness made Him become the perfect sacrificial Lamb who could die for the sins of the world. It is through the sacrifice He made with his blood on the cross that sinners are justified as innocent and righteous in Christ through faith. God reigns in righteousness and justice and expects us to align our lives and conduct with his righteous reign.

God's Righteous Reign Demands Human Righteous Conduct

Brief reflection on the Old Testament righteousness:

In the Old Testament, righteousness requires obeying all the Ten Commandments. Deuteronomy 6:25 says, "And if we are careful to obey all the law before the LORD our God, as he has commanded us, that will be our righteousness". Since it was impossible for mankind to keep all the Ten Commandments, the sacrificial system was provided as the means through which sins were atoned for. Animals were used for atonement of sins. However the Old Testament sacrificial system could not ultimately provide true atonement because it is impossible for the blood of bulls and goats to take away sins (Heb. 10:4). Hence God sent his son as an atoning sacrifice for our sins (1 John 4:10) because Christ earthly life shows that he is the only sinless person who has ever lived (2 Cor. 5:21). Atonement in the New Testament is the reconciliation of God and mankind through the death of Jesus Christ. Jesus' atoning sacrifice by his death on the cross ended the Old Testament sacrificial system.

Brief reflection on the New Testament righteousness:

Christ expanded the requirements of righteousness in His sermon on the mount (Matt. 5-7). Christ did not come to abolish the Law (Ten Commandments) but to fulfill them (Matt. 5:17-18). Through faith in Jesus we become the righteousness of God. Righteousness is part of the fruit believers are expected to bear. God reigns in righteousness and justice. Righteousness and justice are the foundation of his throne (Ps. 97:2, Ps. 89:14). Humans are expected to align their conduct with God's righteous reign. God looks at human righteousness on individual merit (Luke 18:9-14).

There is no act of righteousness that is wasted because God rewards every act of righteousness (Matt. 10:41-42). Righteousness is a contrast to wickedness and must be put into action (Rom. 2:13). Righteousness is related to personal conduct (1 Thess. 2:10) and generally includes love, mercy, kindness, faithfulness, goodness, standing for the truth and what is right, personal uprightness, self-control, perseverance, integrity, selflessness, concern for the marginalized, concern for the poor and needy. For humans to align their conduct with God's righteous reign, means we must guard our godliness at all costs. Believers cannot be sinless but our lives and personal conduct must be seen to be changing through the word of God. We must be men who repent daily and never give up the daily struggle against sins, the world and its desires and against the devil. Pursuing righteousness is one of the examples of carrying the cross to follow Jesus Christ because the cross is a symbol of sacrificial love, obedience and selflessness. When we pursue righteousness, we become messengers of Christ and our lives and personal conduct speak for Jesus.

Righteousness through Faith

The whole purpose of righteousness is for mankind to be in conformity to the person of God and His will, in terms of moral uprightness, justice, faithfulness and integrity. Righteousness and justice are the foundation of God's throne (Ps. 97:2). God's righteousness is divine righteousness (sinless and holy) and key to his saving activity. Mankind cannot be saved through human righteousness which is described in Isaiah 64:6 as "filthy rags". Job questions "How can a man be righteous before God? How can a man born of a woman be pure (Job 25:4)? Romans 3:10, 23 says, "There is no one righteous, not even one. For all have sinned and fall short of the glory of God". Therefore none of us is good enough to earn God's righteousness. Salvation is only possible through God's righteousness. Hence Jesus fulfilled God's righteousness because he demonstrated complete conformity to the nature and will of God (1 Peter 3:18). Salvation is found in no one else; for there is no other name under heaven given to men by which we must be saved (Acts 4:12). Sin separates the relationship God wants to have with mankind. The sacrificial system restores the relationship between God and mankind.

In the Old Testament sin was atoned by the sacrificial system, using the blood of animals. Ultimately, the Old Testament sacrificial system could not provide true atonement because it is impossible for the blood of bulls and goats to take away sins (Heb. 10:4). Therefore God sent his only son Jesus Christ as the atoning sacrificial Lamb for the sins of the world once for all (1 John 4:10). Christ's earthly life shows that He is the only sinless person who has ever lived (2 Cor. 5:21). As the blood of animals could not adequately deal with sins, Jesus became the sacrificial Lamb whose blood purifies humanity from sin (John 1:29, 36; 1 John 1:7). In Jesus we become the righteousness of God (2 Cor. 5:21). The righteousness from God comes through faith in Jesus Christ to all who believe (Rom. 3:22). God's righteousness is a gift through the death of Jesus on the cross. When the kindness and the love of God our saviour appeared, he saved us, not because of righteous things we had done, but because of his mercy (Titus 3:4-5). It is faith righteousness. Faith must be followed with deeds. James 2:14, 17 says, "What good is it my brothers if a man claims to have faith but has no deeds? Can such faith save him? In the same way, faith by itself, if it is not accompanied by action is dead". A person is justified by what he does and not by faith alone (James 2:24). James 2:25-26 says, "In the same way, was not even Rahab the prostitute considered righteous for what she did when she gave lodging to the spies and sent them off in a different direction? As the body without the spirit is dead, so faith without deeds is dead". Mathew 7:20-21 says, "By their fruit you will recognise them. Not everyone who says to me, Lord, Lord, will enter the kingdom of heaven, but only he who does the will of my Father who is in heaven".

Righteousness Cannot Be Exchanged With Tithes, Offerings, Gifts or Donations

In a world which is fast sliding into ungodliness and materialism, preaching and sharing of the message of righteousness have

15

become very necessary. Generally, churches have not given adequate attention to the message of pursuing righteousness compared to preaching about tithing, offerings, breakthrough, deliverance and healing. People go to church mostly because of the following needs such as spiritual, emotional, mental, physical and financial needs. Tithing and offerings are necessary to run and provide for the services of the church. However, the preaching of righteousness in a world that is fast sliding into ungodliness and materialism, the message of righteousness and sin (wickedness) cannot be sidelined or watered down because of the drive for membership and patronage. What people hear on the pulpit is what they apply in their spiritual growth, faith and personal conduct. The message of righteousness will help reduce corruption, murder, wickedness and other vices plaguing the world. In a world without compassion, mercy, love and where winner takes all, the message of righteousness cannot be overemphasised. Tithing, offerings without also pursuing righteousness are condemned by our Lord Jesus Christ (Matt. 23:23). Mark 12:33 says, "To love him with all your heart, with all your understanding and with all your strength, and to love your neighbour as yourself is more important than all your burnt offerings and sacrifices". Amos used an ironic expression to show that tithing cannot replace righteousness (Amos 4:4). In Mathew 23:23, Jesus says, "Woe to you, teachers of the law and Pharisees, you hypocrites. You give a tenth of your spices – mint, dill and cumin. But you have neglected the more important matters of the law – justice, mercy, faithfulness. You should have practised the latter, without neglecting the former". The act of righteousness comes with rewards as the next topic would show. People who do not pursue righteousness would lose out on such rewards. Hence the message of righteousness must be pursued by the church. When we pursue righteousness, we choose to be light in the midst of darkness. The message of righteousness is what will fulfill what Malachi 3:3 says, "Then the Lord will have men who will bring offerings in righteousness".

Challenges in Standing for the Truth and What Is Right

Pursuing righteousness is standing for the truth and what is right no matter what it costs to do so. Ultimately it translates into putting God first in our lives and personal conduct. It means conducting ourselves in a manner worthy of the gospel of Christ, be it in the workplace, offices, in our homes, communities, business, career, vocation and so on. There are times we may be compelled to take a minority position for the sake of standing for the truth and what is right. The Psalmist in Ps. 37:30-31 says. "The mouth of the righteous man utters wisdom and his tongue speaks what is just. The Law of his God is in his heart. His feet do not slip". In an ungodly world, standing for the truth and what is right often come with the risk of stepping on powerful toes. These are realities that we cannot afford to sideline. The consequences could lead to hurting our career progression, disciplinary action, reduction in benefits and perks, discrimination, marginalisation, name calling. You could be re-assigned to a new job or your job description may change, you may be asked to relocate to another department for special duties without any job description. In the worst case scenario, standing for the truth and what is right could end up in termination of appointment.

How Do We Stand Firm in the Midst of Such Challenges?

First and foremost, we must always remember that God overcomes all obstacles. He will deliver us out of troubles when we call upon him (1 Cor. 10:13; 2 Cor. 4:8-9). We are advised to be anxious for nothing but in everything we should give thanks to God through prayers. We must be on the track of faith, trust, prayer, hope and love. In the periods of uncertainty and trials, we are distracted by worrying, fear, anxiety. Christ constantly encourages us to cast our cares upon him and take his yoke upon ourselves in exchange for our burdens (Matt. 11:28-30). Proverbs 18:10 says, "The name of the LORD is a strong tower, the righteous run to it and are saved". There is always peace in the midst of a storm when we put our faith in Jesus Christ. We should pray for those who hurt us (Matt. 5:44). It is the path to victory over persecution and unjust suffering.

The Bible is the word of God and the authoritative guide for all of us. It is one of the greatest resources believers have but it has been under-utilised. All we need in difficult times, all we need for our children, all we need for our marriage, all we need for our families, all we need for our security, all we need for our spiritual growth, faith and conduct are in the Bible. In time of difficulties, Apostle Paul's letter to the Ephesians 6:10-11,14,12-13 says, "Finally be strong in the Lord and in his mighty power. Put on the full armour of God so that you can take your stand against the devil's schemes. Stand firm then, with the belt of truth buckled round your waist, with the breastplate of righteousness in place. For our struggle is not against flesh and blood, but against the rulers, against the authorities, against the powers of this dark world and against the spiritual forces of evil in the heavenly realms. Therefore put on the full armour of God, so that when the day of evil comes, you may be able to stand your ground and after you have done everything to stand". Revelation 17:14 says, "They will make war against the Lamb, but the Lamb will overcome them because He is Lord of lords and King of kings".

Despite the fact that human righteous acts are like filthy rags (Isa. 64:6) still God wants humans to align their conduct with His righteous reign (Rom. 14:17). 1 Peter 2:24 says, "He himself bore our sins in His body on the tree, so that we might die to sins and to live for righteousness". Apostle Paul's letter to Timothy, 2 Tim. 2:22 says, "Flee the evil desires of youth, and pursue righteousness, faith, love, and peace, along with those who call on the Lord out of pure heart". Let us then approach the throne of grace with confidence so that we may receive mercy and find grace to help us in our time of need (Heb. 4:16). Finally, I will close this topic by quoting what Jesus says about those who pursue righteousness in Mathew 5:10. He says, "Blessed are those who are persecuted because of righteousness, for theirs is the kingdom of God".

The Word of Spirit and of Power to Help Us Persevere When Pursuing Righteousness

2 Timothy 3:12

In fact, everyone who wants to live a godly life in Christ Jesus will be persecuted.

James 4:4

Anyone who chooses to be a friend of the world becomes an enemy of God.

1 John 2:15-17

Do not love the world or anything in the world. If anyone loves the world the love of the Father is not in him. For everything in the world – the cravings of the sinful man, the lust of his eyes and the boasting of what he has and does – comes not from the Father but from the world. The world and its desires pass away, but the man who does the will of God lives forever.

John 15:18-20

If the world hates you, keep in mind that it hated me first. If you belonged to the world, it would love you as its own. As it is, you do not belong to the world, but I have chosen you out of the world. This is why the world hates you. Remember the words I spoke to you: No servant is greater than his master. If they persecuted me, they will persecute you also. If they obeyed my teaching, they will obey yours also.

John 17:14-15

I have given them your word and the world has hated them, for they are not of the world any more than I am of the world. My prayer is not that you take them out of the world but that you protect them from the evil one.

Romans 12:12

Be joyful in hope, patient in affliction, faithful in prayer.

Isaiah 14:10

Do not fear, for I am with you; do not be dismayed for I am your God. I will strengthen you and help you; I will uphold you with my righteous hand.

Isaiah 25:4

You have been a refuge for the poor, a refuge for the needy in distress, a shelter from the storm and a shade from the heat. For the breath of the ruthless is like a storm driving agaist a wall.

Psalm 91:1

He who dwells in the shelter of the Most High will rest in the shadow of the Almighty.

Psalm 46:1-3

God is our refuge and strength, an ever present help in trouble. Therefore we will not fear, though the earth give way and the mountains fall into the heart of the sea, though its waters roar and foam and the mountains quake with their surging.

1 Corinthians 7:31

Use the things of the world as if not engrossed in them. For this world in its present form is passing away.

Mark 8:36

What good is it for a man to gain the whole world, yet forfeit his soul?

1 Peter 2:19-21, 23

For it is commendable if a man bears up under the pain of unjust suffering because he is conscious of God. But how is it to your credit if you receive a beating for doing wrong and endure it? But if you suffer for doing good and you endure it, this is commendable before God. To this you were called, because Christ suffered for you, leaving you an example that you should follow in his steps.

20

1 Peter 4:14-16

If you are insulted because of the name Christ, you are blessed, for the Spirit of glory and of God rest on you. If you suffer, it should not be as a murderer or thief or any kind of criminal or even as meddler. However, if you suffer as a Christian, do not be ashamed, but praise God that you bear that name.

Philippians 1:29

For it has been granted to you on behalf of Christ not to only to believe in him but also to suffer for him.

2 Timothy 2:12

If we endure we will also reign with him.

2 Corinthians 1:5

For just as the sufferings of Christ flow over into our lives, so also through Christ our comfort overflows.

Does Righteousness Mean Sinless?

Ordinarily, righteousness could be interpreted as sinless. However, true righteousness means sinless and this is only attributed to God's righteousness. Christ's earthly life shows that he is the only sinless person who has ever lived (2 Cor. 5:21). Humans can only acquire true righteousness which is God's righteousness through faith in Christ Jesus. Human righteousness does not mean sinless but very importantly, because God reigns in righteousness, humans are expected to pursue righteousness. In Luke 18:19, Jesus says, "Why do you call me good? No one is good except God". Isaiah 64:6 says, "All have become like one who is unclean, and all our righteous acts are like filthy rags". Job 25:4 says, "How can a man be righteous before God? How can one born of woman be pure?" Even those prominent names in the Bible who were after the heart of God at some point sinned (Isa. 53:6). For example Noah became drunk (Gen. 9:20-21), Abraham lied to the Egyptians (Gen. 12:13), Jacob lied to his father Isaac (Gen. 27:24), Joshua made a treaty of peace without consulting God (Josh. 9:14-15), rash words came out from Moses lips (Ps. 106:33), David committed adultery and murder (1 Kings 15:5). A good and typical example to show that righteousness does not mean sinless is the kindness and mercy shown by Rahab, the prostitute who helped to hide the Israel's spies and provided safety for them (James 2:25), a risk that could have cost her life. It was credited to her as righteous. For those who claim self-righteousness this may not be apparent to them because they believe in the flesh and not the spirit. They believe in their self-righteousness and not God's righteousness. Christians cannot be sinless but must seek daily repentance. We must be people whose lives are being changed by the Bible (the word of God). We must not give up the daily struggle against sins, the world and its desires, and against the devil. The fact that righteousness does not mean sinless does not give us the authority to live in sin or continue in sin. Finally, I want to encourage ourselves to rise from the ashes of defeat caused by the sinful nature and claim our sonship made possible through faith in Christ Jesus. He is a faithful God and has provided for us unlimited access to seek repentance and forgiveness.

Self-Righteousness

Self-righteousness is righteousness derived from obeying the law and not righteousness that comes through grace and faith in Jesus. Self-righteousness is self-arrogated or self-acclaimed. There is no kingdom value for self-righteousness because salvation is not possible through self-righteousness. The mission of Jesus is to save sinners rather than the "righteous" (Mark 2:17). Jesus strongly questions the righteousness of "the righteous" who are the teachers of the law and the Pharisees who claim to be more righteous. To these groups of self-righteousness, Jesus says in Mark 2:17, "It is not the healthy who need a doctor but the sick. I have not come to call the righteous but sinners". To the group of self-righteous, Apostle Paul in Romans 10:3 says, "Since they did not know the righteousness that comes from God and sought to establish their own, they did not submit to God's righteousness". Self-righteousness relate to people who put their confidence in the righteousness that comes through the flesh rather than God's righteousness. The parable of the Pharisees and tax collector in Luke 18:9-14 is a typical example of self-righteousness. To some who are confident of their own righteousness and looked down on everybody else, Jesus told this parable. "Two men went up to the temple to pray, one a Pharisee, and the other a tax collector. The Pharisee stood up and prayed about himself. God I thank you that I am not like the other men – robbers, evil doers, adulterers – or even like the tax collector. I fast twice a week and give a tenth of all I get. But the tax collector stood at a distance. He would not even look up to heaven, but beat his breast and said, God have mercy on me, a sinner. I tell you that this man, rather than the other, went home justified before God. For everyone who exalts himself will be humbled, and he who humbles himself will be exalted". Galatians 3:11 says, "Clearly no one is justified before God by the law because the righteous will live by faith". Romans 3:20-22 says, "Therefore no one will be declared righteous in his sight by obeying the law rather through the law we become conscious of sin". 1 John 1:8-9 says, "If we claim to be without sin, we deceive ourselves and the truth is not in us. If we confess our sins, he is faithful and just and will forgive us our sins and purify us from all unrighteousness".

The Word of Spirit and of Power

Psalm 143:2

Do not bring your servant into judgment for no-one living is righteous before God.

Isaiah 64:6

All of us have become like one who is unclean, and all our righteous acts are like filthy rags; we all shrivel up like a leaf and like the wind our sins sweep us away.

23

Job 4:17

Can a mortal be more righteous than God? Can a man be more pure than his maker?

Job 25:4

How then can a man be righteous before God? How can one born of a woman be pure?

Romans 10:3

Since they did not know the righteousness that comes from God and sought to establish their own, they did not submit to God's righteousness.

Philippians 3:4-6

If anyone else thinks he has reasons to put confidence in the flesh, I have more; circumcised on the eight day, of the people of Israel, of the tribe of Benjamin, a Hebrew of Hebrews; in regard to the law, a Pharisee; as for zeal, persecuting the church, as for legalistic righteousness, faultless.

Ecclesiastes 7:20

There is not a righteous man on earth who does what is right and never sins.

Luke 18:19

Why do you call me good? No one is good except God alone.

Mathew 23:23

Woe to you, teachers of the Law and Pharisees, you hypocrites. You give a tenth of your spices – mint, dill and cumin. But you have neglected the more important matters of the law – justice, mercy, faithfulness. You should have practised the latter, without neglecting the former.

Luke 11:42

Woe to you Pharisees, because you give God a tenth of your mint, rue and all other kinds of garden herbs, but you neglect justice and the love of God. You should have practised the latter without leaving the former undone.

Galatians 2:16

Know that a man is not justified by observing the law, but by faith in Jesus Christ. So we, too have put our faith in Christ and not by observing the law, because by observing the law no-one will be justified.

James 2:10

For whoever keeps the whole law and yet stumbles at just one point is guilty of breaking all of it.

God Rewards Righteous People

There is no act of righteousness that is wasted. Acts of righteousness will help us share our Christian faith with those around us.

Benefits of righteousness:

The fruit of righteousness will be peace; the effect of righteousness will be quietness and confidence for ever (Isa. 32:17). The LORD detests the sacrifice of the wicked but the prayer of the upright pleases him. The LORD detests the way of the wicked but he loves those who pursue righteousness (Prov. 15:8-9). The account of Noah in 2 Peter 2:4-9, provides a good example of how God rewards righteousness. Noah's righteousness saved him when God brought the flood on the ungodly but protected Noah. Rahab the prostitute enjoyed the fruit of her righteousness also in the land of the living because when the Israelites burned the city of Jericho and everything in it, her family members including everything that belonged to her were spared (Josh 6:22-25). Even in darkness, light dawns for the upright (Ps. 112:4). Light is shed upon the righteous and joy on the upright in heart (Ps. 97:11). A righteous man may have many troubles, but the LORD delivers him from them all (Ps. 34:19). The LORD watches over the way of the righteous but the way of the wicked will perish (Ps. 1:6). Cast your cares on the LORD and he will sustain you; He will never let the righteous fall (Ps. 55:22). For surely O LORD, you bless the righteous; you surround them with your favour as with a shield (Ps. 5:12). Rejoice in the LORD and be glad you righteous; sing all you who are upright in heart (Ps. 32:11). God will meet all our needs according to the glorious riches in Christ Jesus (Phil. 4:19), but we have to seek first his kingdom and his righteousness and all these things will be given to us as well (Matt. 6:33). The wicked man earns deceptive wages, but he who sows righteousness reaps a sure reward (Prov. 11:18). If anyone gives even a cup of cold water to one of these little ones because he is my disciple, I tell you the truth, he will certainly not lose his reward (Matt. 10:42). God is not unjust; he will not forget your work and the love you have shown him as you have helped his people and continue to help them (Heb. 6:10). Do not be deceived, God cannot be mocked. A man reaps what he sows (Gal. 6:7). I was young and now I am old, yet I have never seen the righteous forsaken or their children begging bread. For the LORD loves the just and will not forsake his faithful ones. They will be protected forever, but the offsprings of the wicked will he cut off (Ps. 37:25, 28). The righteous will flourish like palm tree, they will grow like a cedar of Lebanon; planted in the house of the LORD, they will flourish in the courts of our God, they will still bear fruit in old age, they will stay fresh and green (Ps. 92:12-14).

Finally, in Mathew 5:10, Christ says, "Blessed are those who are persecuted because of righteousness, for theirs is the kingdom of heaven". The following scriptures show that God rewards righteousness according to individual merits. 2 Samuel 22:21 says, "The LORD has dealt with me according to my righteousness; according to the cleanness of my hands he has rewarded me". 2 Samuel 22:25 says, "The LORD has rewarded me according to my righteousness, according to my cleanness in his sight". Psalm 7:8 says, "Let the LORD Judge the peoples, judge me, O LORD, according to my righteousness, according to my integrity, O Most High". 1 Samuel 26:23 says, "The LORD rewards every man for his righteousness and faithfulness. The LORD gave you into my hands today, but I would not lay a hand on the LORD's anointed".

The Bible is the authoritative guide for all believers. It is the word of Spirit and of Power, breathed by God and inspired by the Holy Spirit. What the Bible says is the absolute truth for our spiritual growth, faith and conduct. As can be seen from the Bible passages reward from pursuing righteousness overflows to our children and grandchildren and are enjoyed in the land of the living and afterwards in heaven. Hebrews 10:23 says, "Let us hold unswervingly to the hope we profess, for he who promises is faithful". Numbers 23:19 says, "God is not a man that he should lie, nor a son of man, that he should change his mind. Does he speak and then not act? Does he promise and not fulfill?" 2 Corinthians 1:20 says, "For no matter how many promises God has made, they are "Yes" in Christ. And so through him, the "Amen" is spoken by us to the glory of God". Joshua 21:45 says, "Not one of all the LORD's good promises to the house of Israel failed. Everyone was fulfilled".

Chapter 4

WHAT DO YOU FORSAKE FOR THE SAKE OF KNOWING CHRIST?

— ✳ —

Firstly, let us reflect on the sacrifice Christ made to bring us close to God. He shed his blood on the cross for the sins of the world (John 1:29). He endured the cross, scorning its shame so that we might be reconciled with God by his blood shed on the cross (Col. 1:20). God's curse on sin is death. Jesus carried God's curse on sin upon himself in order to free us from that curse. Galatians 3:13 says, "Christ redeemed us from the curse of the law by becoming a curse for us", for it is written "cursed is everyone who is hung on a tree". Considering the weight of the sacrifice he made for me and you, the question is, what sacrifice can we also make for him? Should it always be what I want from Jesus? Should it always be about me, me, me? What do you forsake for the sake of knowing Jesus? What sacrifice do you make that put Christ first rather than your personal interest in your home, in your community, in your workplace, in the market place and so on. For example, Moses chose to be ill-treated along with the people of God rather than to enjoy the pleasures of sin for a short time. He accepted disgrace for the sake of Christ as of greater value than the treasures of Egypt (Heb. 11:25-26). By faith he left Egypt, not fearing the king's anger; he persevered because he saw him who is invisible (Heb. 11:27). Acts 5:41 says, "The Apostles left the Sanhedrin, rejoicing because they had been counted worthy of suffering disgrace for the Name".

In Apostle Paul's letter to the Philippians (Phil. 3:7-9) he says, "Whatever was to my profit I now consider loss for the sake of

Christ. What is more, I consider everything a loss compared to the surpassing greatness of knowing Christ my Lord for whose sake I have lost all things. I consider them rubbish that I may gain Christ and be found in him." It is through the blood of Jesus that we have confidence to enter the Most Holy Place (Heb. 10:19). Our lives should speak for Jesus. Offerings, tithing and donations are encouraged but they cannot replace righteousness (Amos 4:4). Our righteous acts speak for Jesus and bring us closer to God. For example, when a person does a good deed when he or she should not have to, God is pleased. The prostitute Rahab who hid the Israelites' spies was credited as righteous for showing mercy (James 2:25). She put God first not minding the great risk to her life for such an action.

The Word of Spirit and of Power

Ephesians 2:10

For we are God's workmanship, created in Christ Jesus to do good works, which God prepared in advance for us to do.

Hebrews 13:12

And so Jesus also suffered outside the city gate to make the people holy through his own blood. Let us, then go to him outside the camp, bearing the disgrace he bore.

Philippians 3:10

I want to know Christ and the power of his resurrection and the fellowship of sharing in his sufferings, becoming like him in his death.

Job 2:10

Shall we accept good from God and not trouble?

1 Peter 4:13

But rejoice that you participate in the suffering of Christ, so that you may be overjoyed when his glory is revealed.

2 Corinthians 1:5

For just as the sufferings of Christ flow over into our lives, so also through Christ our comfort overflows.

1 Peter 2:19, 21

For it is commendable if a man bears up under the pain of unjust suffering because he is conscious of God. To this you were called, because Christ suffered for you, leaving you an example that you should follow in his steps.

Isaiah 50:6

I offered my back to those who beat me, my cheeks to those who pulled out my beard. I did not hide my face from mocking and spitting.

Chapter 5

BRIEF REFLECTION ON
THE MINISTRY

---※---

All believers are in the ministry of Jesus. The church, the members, the workers and all believers in various vocations are all in the ministry's work. Everyone is important and equal before God. The ministry, from the publicity point of view has been well publicised compared to the past. This has been made possible as a result of modern communication technology. However, in terms of the things of God, the effect of the improved publicity of the ministry on society has not been successful, considering that the world is fast sliding towards materialism and ungodliness (spiritual darkness). The improved publicity is yet to make any meaningful impact. A positive response to this unacceptable situation would be to strengthen the structure of the ministry which can be expressed in the following areas:

1. General ministry
2. Focused ministry
3. Only one major area of ministry
4. Varieties of ministries.

In a world which is fast becoming ungodly, I see the focused ministry playing a very strong role in the work of the ministry especially considering that the focused ministry can be spread across wide areas such as:

1. Ministry through the structure of society.
2. Ministry through one's vocation.

3. Ministry through the needy areas of society.
4. Ministry through the organisational life of the church.

The four areas of focused ministry are avenues and channels for personal contacts and interactions where believers can showcase or demonstrate their Christ-like character. For example, believers interact with society through their vocations such as in the workplace, offices, factories, social life, marketplace, educational institutions such as schools, colleges and institutions of higher learning, meetings, conferences, sporting life, health centers and many more. Such interactions provide opportunity for sharing their Christian faith with people around them. If you are a true believer, you will be a better wife, husband, student, teacher, pastor, lecturer, accountant, judge, lawyer, engineer, doctor, and through these channels you can impact society through your Christ-like new life (new heart, new mind and new self (Eph. 4:22-24)).

The ministry through the organisational life of the church is also a very strong area for personal and group interactions with society. The organisational life of the church can be expressed in the following areas, such as evangelism, women's and men's associations, prayer groups, welfare groups, outreach groups, youth groups, fellowship groups and so on.

The church and every believer can also impact the world through the needy areas of society. In the past, the church and other Christian organisations have used channels, such as ownership of schools, colleges, universities and hospitals, to promote the work of the ministry. I attended both an Anglican primary school and an Anglican grammar school. I thank God that I did. These institutions shaped my life in the fear of God. Educational institutions and hospitals established by Christian organisations are focused avenues for Christian faith sharing which promotes the work of the ministry towards the needy area of society. The church and other Christian organisations have also invested in the needy areas of society through ownership of low-cost accommodation, such as hostels for students and tourists who cannot afford the high cost of hostels and private accommodations. Finally, every believer is expected to live a life of generosity. We cannot talk of God's generosity without also being generous with the little we have. In Hebrews 13:16; 6:10 believers are advised not to forget to do good and to share with others, for with such sacrifices God is pleased. God is not unjust; he will not forget your work and the love you have shown him as you have helped his people and continue to help them. Wealth and riches come with the duty to give generously to those in need (Prov. 11:24-25). Every believer is in the ministry of Jesus. The church and every believer have the responsibility to promote the work of the ministry. There are people who will go to hell because we have failed. A chain is only strong at its weakest point. The weakest point in the church may be you in spreading the gospel through your personal examples (Christlikeness and new nature). Christianity is about change. The change you have received through your new nature should touch the lives of those around you through your examples. You cannot share your Christian faith with people and expect them to ignore your examples.

Chapter 6

CALL TO SERVE

❋

Calling is the modern name for invitation. Each of us has specific calling. Specific calling is about travelling on the road that God has asked you to travel (Col. 1:24-29). To serve the Lord faithfully with gladness (Eph. 4:16) is serving for the kingdom's purpose. It is a call to serve as against volunteering which means I am doing you a favour and this is different from serving. Jesus is our saviour and king. He gave his life to pay for our sins and to serve him faithfully with passion will change the world. To serve means you are called to serve in God's army, doing His will, God's way. Use your gift to serve with passion. The crowd needs God's grace (Joel 3:14). People who know that they have been forgiven serve best (Deut. 28:47-48). Serving is the same as works. James 2:26 says, "As the body without the spirit is dead, so faith without deeds is dead". Faith without works is dead. Joshua said, "As for me and my household; we will serve the LORD" (Josh. 24:15). Serve the king with gladness. To serve is a manifestation of Christianity; Jesus served.

Set Personal Examples

Personal examples while serving are helpful in spreading the good news. Believers should not expect those around them to accept their advice and ignore their personal examples. Believers should set personal examples while serving. In Apostle Paul's letter to Titus (Titus 2:7-8), he says "In everything set them an example by doing what is good. In your teaching, show integrity, seriousness, and soundness of speech that cannot be condemned so that those who oppose you may be ashamed because they have nothing bad to say about us". "Let your light shine before men that they may see your good deeds and praise your father in Heaven" (Matt. 5:16).

The Baton

Jesus passed the baton to his twelve disciples. The baton is also in our hands. The baton is the good news and we have it in our hands. There are people who will go to hell because you have failed. A chain is only strong at its weakest point. The weakest point in the church may be you in spreading the gospel through your personal examples.

The good news should affect your life and transform it into the new nature. Christianity is about change. Take the new nature into your community, workplace, sporting life, market place, professional life, business life, fishing community, farming community and other places wherever you find yourselves. Make good use of every opportunity.

Sharing the Word of God

The personalities of those who preach the Bible are not the same. They have different ways of getting the message across. They also have different skills such as communication skills and persuasion skills. They are expected not to put their confidence in their skills or self-righteousness. Instead they should put their confidence in God who breathed the Bible. Sharing the word is about helping people to understand the word of God. Clarity is required in pressing the truth home to the hearts of ourselves and those listening. Those sharing the word of God are therefore challenged by getting the message right and getting it across to the listeners. Hence it is very necessary that they must have great understanding of the Bible passage and how to communicate the truth effectively. Watering down of the message must be avoided because that would translate to watering down the truth. Jesus did not water down his message in order to attract hearers.

The preaching duty is not all that is involved in sharing the word of God as the next discussions show.

Godly Living Promotes the Ministry

Preachers and those who share the word of God should guard their lives and live godly lives. It is God's appointed way to bring His truth to human hearts through human beings, who are themselves being transformed by that truth. Paul tells Timothy to devote himself to the public reading of the scripture, "to preaching and teaching". He tells him, "Be diligent in these matters; give yourself wholly to them, so that everyone may see your progress". But in case Timothy thinks he is just to work at sermon preparation, Paul goes on, "watch your life and doctrine closely" (1Tim. 4:13-16). His godliness is to be guarded at all costs. Timothy cannot be sinless, but must be a man whose life is being changed by God through the Bible he preaches. He must be a man who repents daily because repentance is a daily experience. He must be a man who never gives up the daily struggle against sin, the world and its desires and the devil. He must be a man who knows that his own Christlikeness is more important than his preaching skills. Advice of Apostle Paul to Timothy also applies to all believers. A preacher or those who share the word of God cannot ask their listeners to accept their preaching or advice and expect them to ignore their personal examples. Integrity is the basis for credible ministry. Watch your life and doctrine carefully.

Pray for the Listeners

Preachers and those who share the word of God must as a formality pray for their listeners. In Thessalonica, the gospel came, "Not simply with words but also with power, with the Holy Spirit and deep conviction" (1 Thess. 1:5). Preaching and sharing of the word are done with words; it cannot be done without words. Thus, we need to pray that along with the Words, the Holy Spirit of God will usher in the listeners a deep conviction that the words are the truth. Preaching and sharing the word of God are like sowing and watering the seed. When you sow and water and the seed did not grow, you should not feel guilty. It is Christ that has the responsibility for saving souls. But do your best to sow and water the seed to grow, supported by prayers. If the listener is not saved, you should not feel guilty as far as you have done your part through discipleship and evangelism. You should leave the rest to God (John 6:44).

Dependence on the Holy Spirit

Sharing the scripture will need complete dependence upon the Holy Spirit of God to shine his light on the scripture passage and ask him to open our blind eyes to see the truth. This is consistent with the Psalmist prayer in Psalm 119:18 which says, "Open my eyes that I may see wonderful things in your law". The Bible is the word of God in a written text by human writers revealed and inspired by God (2 Tim. 3:16-17). God is the ultimate Author of the Bible. It is the word of Spirit and of Power. It is through prayer that preachers and those who share the word of God can ask for the Spirit of God to guide them and help them in the right understanding of the Bible. This attitude should not be taken as a formality but as needful.

All Believers are in the Ministry of Jesus

The work of preachers is not different from others. Despite the fact that the preacher stands in the middle between God and the people, the work of the preacher in the New Testament is not different from that of any other worker or a school teacher. The work of the preacher should not be seen as holier. Everyone is doing what God has called him to do. God in all I do let me honour you (Col. 3:23-25). 1 Peter 4:11 says, "If anyone speaks, he should do it as one speaking the very words of God. If anyone serves, he should do it with the strength God provides, so that in all things God may be praised through Jesus Christ".

Take the Bible into your life. The Bible should affect your everyday life, how you work, how you talk, your body language, your character and so on. Everyone is important before God. Christianity is about change. As soon as you have accepted Christ, people should see change in your life. You should be seen as doing the will of God from the heart. When opportunity comes, make Christ known. Christianity should make you a better wife, a better husband, a better worker, a better community leader, a better student, and so on. Always share your testimony to help people come to Christ.

Avoid Distorting the Word

The Bible is a perfect and complete book inspired and breathed by God. It is an authoritative proclamation from God to us that must be obeyed, that must be sought, and that cannot be ignored. Modern life, time and culture differences should not have any impact on the word of God. Improvement in the language to help understanding can go on from time to time without compromising on the contents, bearing in mind that it is the Holy Spirit that helps believers in the understanding of the Bible.

It remains possible for those who preach or share the word of God to distort and manipulate the "Word" of God for their selfish ends. Such is possible through ignoring the content of a passage, mistranslating a word or phrase by importing own assumptions into the text, by failing to relate what we read to the center of the Bible which is the gospel of Jesus Christ, the crucified and risen saviour, who is and always will be the Lord of Heaven and Earth. If that happens, we can end up with a very different word which has no power and no authority. We cannot be taking God seriously if we do not take the "Word" seriously. The Bible bears God's own authority. We need to "Correctly handle the Word of truth" (2 Tim. 2:15). The Bible is the story of real people and real places inspired by the Holy Spirit in written form. It is forbidden to play around with it.

Serving Faithfully with our Talents

Christ expects believers to use their specific talents and opportunities he has given them to serve the Lord. They are expected to serve faithfully with their talents and gifts. To each one, the manifestation of the spirit is given for the common good

(1 Cor. 12:7). Each one should use whatever gift he has received to serve others faithfully, administering God's grace in its various forms (1 Peter 4:10). It is required that those who have been given a trust must prove faithful (1 Cor. 4:2). From everyone who has been given much, much will be demanded; and from those who have been entrusted with much, much more will be asked (Luke 12:48).

Total Allegiance

James reminds us that God is a jealous God who rightfully demands total allegiance (Deut. 4:24; James 4:5). The fundamental sin then is for people to be "double minded" (James 1:8, 4:8). The temptation to try to be friends with God and friends with the world at the same time is nothing less than spiritual adultery (James 4:4). If we are faithful, God remains faithful. In serving God, He wants first place in our lives. One of God's attributes is jealousy. God is jealous. He rightly demands our loyalty over everything. Family, church, friends, career, hobbies, holidays, recreation, are good and necessary, but they should not be ranked before God. We should put God first in whatever we do in our churches, in our families, friendship, careers, hobbies, holidays, recreations and so on. There are people who need love, mercy, kindness, compassion, justice and so on. How do we factor them into our daily living? Just as well, many villages, towns, cities, and nations are not in peace. Due to the pandemic, many villages, towns, cities around the world are being ravaged by poverty and shortage of medical supplies aggravated by non-availability of covid-19 vaccines. How do we as Christians factor these into our daily lives?

Rewards and Discipline

God rewards and disciplines but His purpose for us remains firm. After the period of David and Solomon, Chronicles divides the lives of Judah's kings into periods of obedience that resulted in God's blessings and disobedience that resulted in His judgment against them. This repeated pattern helps to remind us that while our eternal salvation is secure in Jesus Christ, God will reward us as we serve him faithfully (Mark 10:29-30). It also reminds us that God will discipline his people, as a father disciplines his children, when we turn from him (Heb. 12:7-11).

The chronicles were written to encourage Israel to move forward after a time of great suffering in exile by assuring them that God's purpose for Israel will never fail. The book of Chronicles is a great encouragement to every believer. Even when we suffer setbacks and disappointments, we can be rest assured that God's purpose for us in Christ Jesus will not fail.

Chapter 7

SERVING GOD IN THE WORKPLACE (FOCUSED MINISTRY)

※

In the book of Genesis, work started with God being the creator of all things (Gen. 1:1). God created all that is. He created light and darkness; sky and earth, sun, moon and stars; land and sea; plant and animal life; and mankind (Gen. 1-2). He is God the worker. He is always working. God's works are good and they include creation (Gen. 2:23; Isa. 40:28), sustenance of the earth (Heb. 1:3) and redemption (Exod. 6:6; Rom. 8:23). He is always working to sustain us and his creation. The Bible reveals Christ as the one through whom God created all things (John 1:1-3; Col. 1:16). Jesus came to do his Father's work (John 5:16-18). He called his disciples to leave their occupations to follow him (Mark 1:14-19). In whatever work believers find themselves in, they should regard themselves as co-workers in God's service (1 Cor. 3:9). We are all in the ministry of Jesus. We must serve him faithfully. Our work and labour are not in vain (1 Cor. 15:58).

Work is performed as service to God (Col. 3:17, 22-24). Work is one way that we fulfill the divine image of God's creation with his command to fill and subdue and rule the Earth which implies work (Gen. 1:26-28). Furthermore, God put the man in the Garden of Eden "to work it and take care of it" (Gen. 2:15). Work is necessary for human dignity as well as for survival. Idleness is condemned (Prov. 12:24; 2 Thess. 3:6-10). Work is a good gift God has given us in creation. On the other hand, unjust working conditions are a cause for worry and they incur God's judgment (Prov. 14:31; James 5:4-6).

The workplace is part of the focused ministry and presents an opportunity to serve and honour God. It is an opportunity to make Christ known through your vocation by sharing your faith demonstrated through your new heart, new mind and new self to those around you. The Bible says, in whatsoever work you are involved in, you must give your best service from your heart to your employer. You should serve him from your heart and render the best service as if you were serving the Lord. Obey your employers not just to attract their favour when their attention is on you, but like slaves of Christ doing the will of God from your heart, knowing that the Lord will reward everyone according to his good work. Work as if you are working for the Lord and not men, since you will receive an inheritance from the Lord as your reward. To give your best to your employer, apply all the resources available for the work solely for accomplishing the work. Your working hours should be used for serving your employers only. Give to Caesar what belongs to Caesar and to God what belongs to God (Eph. 6:5-8; Col. 3:23-25; Matt. 22:19-21).

Every Worker is in the Ministry

Every one of us is in the ministry. Do not see the work of the preacher or the evangelist as holier than any other worker or the teacher. They are all doing what God has called them to do. What is important is to honour God in all you do. The message is take the Bible into your life. The Bible should affect your everyday life. Let the Bible affect how you do your work, how you talk, how you walk, how you relate to your boss, your subordinates (staff) and other workers. Everyone is important to Christ. Christianity is about change. As soon as you have accepted Christ, people should see change in your life. It is an opportunity to display Christ's nature at your job. Doing the will of God from your heart is what counts. Christianity will make you a better wife, a better husband, a better accountant, a better engineer, a better teacher, a better student, a better pharmacist and so on. Do not do anything that will compromise your walk with God. Do not expect your fellow workers to accept your doctrine and ignore your example. Work as one in the light.

Resist Reading the Bible during the Hours of Work

Giving your best to your employer is one of the best investments you can make for God and expect his reward. Avoid anything that will distract you from putting in your best for your employer. Do not use your employer's working hours to read the Bible or hold Bible fellowships. Follow what the scripture says, "Give to Caesar what is Caesar's and to God what is God's" (Matt. 22:21). However, if your employer approves of it, then that becomes part of the working policy. Bible reading and fellowship can be accommodated during tea break and lunch time. You should watch out that the work hours are not compromised because if you use your lunch time for fellowship or reading the Bible, you may be tempted to encroach on your work time to have your lunch. Ultimately that is likely to affect your work performance. Even when you have completed your work and you have some time to spare, since it is within the working hours, it would be advisable to spend that time to seek for better ways to improve your work.

Think About This:

Reading the Bible during work hours gives a divided attention and could lead to failing to relate what we read to what God is saying to us. Random or casual reading of the Bible will not change us unless we are learning and understanding something. The Bible carries God's own authority. Only by seriously studying these words will we become wise for salvation through faith in Jesus Christ. The Bible is the word of truth. We need to rightly handle it as it has everything we need for faith and conduct. Resist the temptation of reading the Bible randomly or with divided attention. Do not allow anything that will compromise your walk with God. What is really important is to take Jesus' nature to your workplace. Let your light shine before your fellow workers that they may see your deeds and praise your Father in Heaven (Matt. 5:16).

My Work Life Experience

I worked for the OPEC organisation in Vienna, Austria for 8 years from 1985 to 1993. In my previous working life, I tried to avoid the temptation of reading the Bible during the working hours set by my employers. Along the line, God has helped me keep to this principle. I do set aside my personal time to study the Bible at home. However, when I travel out on duty, I read my Bible on the plane and in the hotel room. When I arrived in Vienna to commence my employment, I maintained this principle. I and my family worshipped at the Vienna International Baptist Church. I was one of the church leaders and I participated in teaching at the Sunday school youth Bible studies, and the weekly youth Bible studies. I and my wife, Grace also hosted Friday late evening church fellowship meetings in my house. I was also the head of the church ushers. My hands were quite full.

Testimony

In the OPEC secretariat, one of my colleagues did set up Bible fellowship meetings during the lunch time. I gave my support but decided not to attend because of my already crowded programme. Adding the lunch time fellowship was therefore not possible for me. On the other hand, one of my colleagues, Flores, a Filipino and a very committed Christian who joined OPEC after I joined, registered to attend the fellowship meetings. He started attending and continued for a while. Surprisingly, during one lunch break he came into my office. I asked why he was not at the fellowship meeting. He informed me that he had stopped attending. I asked for the reason why he stopped. His reason was that the fellowship time was in conflict with his official working time. His job was adversely being affected, because he spent his lunch time at the fellowship and afterwards struggled to find something to eat during his work time. He said it affected his conscience and now he knows why I had not accepted to be part of the fellowship. I told him that my programme for the day was already loaded. We discussed further and he checked on other fellowship programmes outside the working time and weekends and he made contact and he joined a more suitable one timewise.

Christian Faith Sharing at the Workplace

Fellowship and prayer meetings at the workplace are good opportunities for sharing the Christian faith, if supported with a suitable time plan to avoid any conflict in the workers giving their best to the employers. The breakfast times, lunch times and tea times are suitable periods for such meetings. Personal examples are critical in successfully sharing one's faith at the workplace across the board as regards your boss, your staff and fellow workers. The best way to share Christian faith is to work hard and demonstrate the peace and love of Christ at the workplace. Office parties also present opportunities to share your Christian faith with others. Christ was not selective in mixing with people (Matt. 9:10). You have responsibility to your boss, your staff and other workers. When you live right among colleagues and those around you, they will easily give you their attention when you need them. For example when I was working in OPEC, I took time to read through the staff handbook, which provides various information for staff to help them in accessing and locating important government agencies, schools, hospitals, religious organisations and their addresses. While I was going through the book, I noticed that the list of churches included were few. I chose an appropriate time to have audience with the head of administration and the personnel head to discuss my intention to request for an increase in the number of churches listed in the staff handbook. I have had a good working relationship with the Secretary General, the head of Administration and the head of Personnel. I had at some point shared my Christian faith with them. When I introduced the matter of making changes to the handbook to include more churches to the head of Administration and head of Personnel, they were very positive about it. It was decided that the head of Administration should write to the Secretary General to obtain his approval, which he easily gave. This ended the initial skepticism by the people around me who thought my request would backfire and would not get approved because those who would give the approval were of a different religion. But they were proven wrong at the end. An effective way to demonstrate our Christian faith in the office is not by reading the Bible but by sharing Christ's love, mercy, kindness, compassion, justice and so on. It is also the best means of sharing our Christian faith with others from a different faith or religion.

The Word of Spirit and of Power

Ephesians 6:5-8

Slaves, obey your earthly masters with respect and fear, and with sincerity of heart, just as you would obey Christ. Obey them not only to win their favour when their eye is on you, but like slaves of Christ, doing the will of God from your heart. Serve wholeheartedly, as if you were serving the Lord not men, because you know that the Lord will reward everyone for whatever good he does, whether he is slave or free.

Colossians 3:23-25

Whatever you do, work at it with all your heart, as working for the Lord, not for men, since you know that you will receive an inheritance from the Lord as a reward. It is the Lord Christ you are serving. Anyone who does wrong will be repaid for his wrong, and there is no favouritism.

2 Thessalonians 3:11-13

We hear that some among you are idle. They are not busy; they are busy-bodies. Such people we command and urge in the Lord Jesus Christ to settle down and earn the bread they eat. And so for you, brothers, never be tired of doing what is right.

Mathew 5:16

In the same way, let your light shine before men, that they may see your good deeds and praise your Father in heaven.

1 Corinthians 3:8

The man who plants and the man who waters have one purpose, and each will be rewarded according to his own labour.

Mathew 22:19-21

"Show me the coin used for paying the tax". They brought him a denarius, and he asked them "Whose portrait is this? And whose inscription?". "Caesar's" they replied. Then he said to them, "Give to Caesar what is Caesar's and to God what is God's."

Titus 2:9-10

Teach slaves to be subject to their masters in everything, to try to please them, not to talk back to them, and not to steal from them, but to show that they can be fully trusted, so that in every way they will make the teaching about God our saviour attractive.

Chapter 8

INTEGRITY IS THE BASIS FOR CREDIBLE MINISTRY

※

As believers we must watch our lives closely and cloth ourselves with godliness. Christlikeness in personal conduct is God's approved way of bringing the word of God to human hearts through humans who are themselves being transformed by the word of God. Believers must guard their godliness at all costs, because they cannot expect those around them to accept their doctrine and ignore their example. Their personal conduct must be above reproach. They must be self-controlled, respectable, upright, blameless, incorruptible and so on. They must hold strongly to moral uprightness, honesty, be trustworthy and so on. A believer cannot be sinless, but must be someone who is being changed by God through the Word of God and is growing in the new nature. He should be someone who repents every day, who never gives up the daily struggle against sin, against the world and its desires and the devil. Paul regularly defended his integrity (1 Thess. 2:9-12). He also encourages Titus to show integrity in his teaching (Titus 2:7). He further instructed Titus and Timothy that as church leaders they must be blameless, sincere and above reproach. They should be people of integrity (Titus 1:6-8; 1 Tim. 3:2-10).

Examples of Individuals of Integrity

Certain individuals in the Bible are described as examples of integrity. Noah was "a righteous man, blameless among the people of his time and he walked with God" (Gen 6:9). Job is described as "blameless and upright; he feared God and shunned evil" (Job 1:1). Daniel is also credited with moral uprightness and being incorruptible. The administrators and the Satraps tried to find grounds for charges against Daniel in his conduct of government affairs, but they were unable to do so. They could find no corruption in him, because he was trustworthy and never corrupt nor negligent. Finally these men said, "We will never find any basis for charges against this man Daniel unless it has something to do with the law of his God" (Daniel 6:4-5).

Desires: Christians Should Watch Out

Believers should watch out for their desires. Ungodly desires affect the ministry of Jesus. Deceitfulness of wealth and desires for the things of the flesh affect the promotion of the ministry. Ungodly desire brought darkness into the world through the sin of the first man, Adam. Christ warns us to be on our guard against all forms of greed because a man's life does not depend on the abundance of his possession (Luke 12:15). Wait on the Lord for the fulfillment of your desires. Always pass your desires through quality control checks. Galatians 5:16 says, "So I say live by the Spirit and you will not gratify the desires of the sinful nature". Check if your desire is to please God or to please the world or to satisfy your selfish interests. Check if the desire runs contrary to what the Bible says or not. Consider the consequences of satisfying desires that go against the word of God. When we accept Christ, we do not need to conform to the pattern of this world any longer. Transformation in our lives starts by the renewing of our minds. Selfish ambition, corruption, greed, perversion of justice, dishonest gains and riches are ungodly desires. If you live by the Spirit, the desires of the sinful nature will be in conflict with the Spirit and you do not do what you want (Gal. 5:16-17). By reading the Bible, you will be led by the Spirit of truth. Before we start reading the Bible, we should always ask God to open our blind eyes to see the truth (Ps. 119:18).

Ungodly desires result in sinning against God and end in disappointments and sometimes in disasters. Such desires make people harbour bitter envy and selfish ambition in their hearts which end up in disorder and very evil practices (James 3:13-17).

Some Examples of Desires That Ended in Disappointments or Disaster

Samuel's sons lost the opportunity to become kings of Israel because of ungodly desires, which included dishonest gains. They accepted bribes and perverted justice. They failed to follow the examples set by their father, Samuel (1 Sam. 8:1, 3).

The elders of Israel wanted a king because the other nations had kings without first seeking for God's approval(1Sam.8:4-8). They came to Samuel to ask for a king. Even after Samuel had told them what the king would do to them, they still went on with their demand and God gave them Saul, the son of Kish(1Sam.8:9-19;10:20-25).

The men of Israel sampled the provisions of the Gibeonites without seeking God's approval. Joshua made peace treaty with them and the leaders of the assembly ratified it by oath without inquiring from God. Three days after the treaty, the Israelites discovered that the Gibeonites were their neighbours. They could not drive away the Gibeonites because the leaders of the assembly swore an oath by the LORD, the God of Israel (Josh. 9:14-18).

Desire to Be Like God

Some have gone to the extent of nursing the desire to be like God. The temptation to usurp God's power is part of such desire. The fall of man in the book of Genesis was a direct result of sin caused by human desire. The first man, Adam disobeyed God by eating the fruit from the forbidden tree in order to have the knowledge of good and evil to fulfill the desire to be like God (Gen. 3:5). His action resulted in very grave consequences for mankind. All the originally perfect relationships with God were broken.

Mankind came under the curse of God's judgment and was no longer justified to stand in God's presence. Mankind became an enemy of God, the land bearing its fruits through a "painful toil" (Gen. 3:17). The darkness of Genesis chapter 3 affected the natural world because of the desire of the first man to take over God's power. Believers should always be in check of their desires by passing them through quality control by following what the Bible says. In living every moment rightly for Jesus, resist the urge to infringe on or usurp God's authority or compromise His authority. Always seek for desires that will honour God.

There are gifts of prophesy in the Bible, but believers should exercise restraint in fulfilling their desires for prophecy so that they do not go contrary to what the Bible says. Such prophecies should be subjected to the authority of the Bible. The desire by prophets in the present age to prophesise about the exact date of Christ's second coming is believing the unbelievable. Jesus coming is not debatable, it is certain but the exact time is unknown because in Matthew 24:36, Jesus himself said, "No one knows about that day or hour, not even the angels in Heaven nor the son, but only the Father".

What Does the Bible Say About Ungodly Desires?

Genesis 3:5

"For God knows that when you eat of it, your eyes will be opened and you will be like God, knowing good and evil".

Genesis 3:17

To Adam he said, "Because you listened to your wife and ate from the tree about which I commanded you, 'You must not eat of it', cursed is the ground because of you; through painful toil you will eat of it all the days of your life".

1 Samuel 8:1, 3

When Samuel grew old, he appointed his sons as judges for Israel. But his sons did not walk in his ways. They turned aside after dishonest gain and accepted bribes and perverted justice.

Joshua 9:14-18

The men of Israel sampled their provisions but did not inquire of the LORD. Then Joshua made a treaty of peace with them to let them live, and the leaders of the assembly ratified it by oath. Three days after they made the treaty with the Gibeonites, the Israelites heard that they were neighbours living near them. So the Israelites set out and on the third day came to their cities; Gibeon, Kephirah, Beeroth and Kiriath Jearim. But the Israelites did not attack them, because the leaders of the assembly had sworn an oath to them by the LORD, the God of Israel.

James 4:2-3

You want something but don't get it. You kill and covet, but you cannot have what you want. You quarrel and fight. You do not have because you do not ask God.

James 3:13-17

Who is wise and understanding among you? Let him show it by his good life, by deeds done in the humility that comes from wisdom. But if you harbour bitter envy and selfish ambition in your hearts, do not boast about it or deny the truth. Such "wisdom" does not come down from heaven but it is earthly, unspiritual, of the devil. For where you have envy and selfish ambition, there you find disorder and every evil practice. But the wisdom that comes from heaven is first of all pure, then peace-loving, considerate, submissive, full of mercy and good fruit, impartial and sincere.

How to Handle Desires:

1. Growing in the New Life

When we accepted Christ, we were buried with him through baptism into death in order that just as Christ was raised from the dead through the glory of the Father, we too may live a new life (Rom. 6:4). If anyone is in Christ, he is a new creation, the old has gone the new has come (2 Cor. 5:17). Do not conform any longer to the pattern of this world, but be transformed by the renewing of your mind. Then you will be able to test and approve what God's will is – his good, pleasing and perfect will (Rom. 12:2).

You were taught with regard to your former way of life, to put off your old self which is being corrupted by its deceitful desires, to be made new in the attitude of your minds; and to put on the new self, created to be like God in true righteousness and holiness (Eph. 4:22-24).

2. Put God First

Watch out for your desires. Put God first in all your desires. Pass your desires to the Lord. Ungodly desires affect the believer's integrity and ultimately the work of the ministry. The desires of the old self make the sinful mind hostile to God. Those controlled by the sinful mind cannot please God (Rom. 8:7-8). Trust in him to supply your needs. He never disappoints. God never lies. His promises are settled. He says, "You will seek me and find me when you seek me with all your heart" (Jer. 29:13). Apostle Paul in Philippians 4:19 says, "My God will meet all your needs according to his glorious riches in Christ Jesus". In Luke 12:15, Christ said, "Watch out! Be on your guard against all kinds of greed; a man's life does not consist in the abundance of his possessions". Jesus assures us in Luke 12:29, 31 "Don't worry about what you will eat, what will you drink, about what will happen tomorrow. But seek his kingdom first and these things will be given to you as well."

What the Bible Says:

Philippians 4:4-7

Rejoice in the Lord always. I will say it again Rejoice! Let your gentleness be evident to all. The Lord is near. Do not be anxious about anything, but in everything, by prayer and petition, with thanksgiving, present yours to God. And the peace of God, which transcends all understanding, will guard your hearts and your minds in Christ Jesus.

Psalm 37:4-7

Delight yourself in the LORD and he will give you the desires of your heart. Commit your way to the LORD; trust in him and he will do this: He will make your righteousness shine like the dawn, the justice of your cause like the noonday sun. Be still before the LORD and wait patiently for him.

3. God Has Assured Us That He Will Meet Our Needs; God Has Our Best at Heart

What the Bible says:

Jeremiah 29:11

For I know the plans I have for you, declares the LORD, "Plans to prosper you and not to harm you, plans to give you hope and a future.

Psalm 84:11

For the LORD God is a sun and shield; the LORD bestows favour and honour; no good thing does he withhold from those whose walk is blameless.

James 1:17

Every good and perfect gift is from above, coming down from the Father of the heavenly lights, who does not change like shifting shadows.

Mathew 7:9-11

Which of you, if his son asks for bread, will give him a stone? Or if he asks for a fish, will give him a snake? If you then, though you are evil, know how to give good gifts to your children, how much more will your father in heaven give good gifts to those who ask him!

4. Trust God for the Best; Be Patient and Wait On the LORD

What the Bible Says:

Acts 13:21-22

Then the people asked for a king and he gave them Saul, son of Kish, of the tribe of Benjamin who ruled for forty years. After removing Saul, he made David their king. He testified concerning him: "I have found David son of Jesse a man after my own heart; he will do everything I want him to do."

Numbers 32:5

If we have found favour in your eyes they said, "Let this land be given to your servants as our possession. Do not make us cross the Jordan."

I Samuel 13:14

But now your kingdom will not endure; the LORD has sought out a man after his own heart and appointed him leader of his people, because you have not kept the LORD's commandment.

5. Pass Your Desires through Quality Control

Desires should be guided by what the Bible says to ensure that they are not hostile to God. Desires born out of selfish motives to satisfy the flesh are hostile to God.

6. The Life of A Man Does Not Consist In the Abundance of His Possessions (Luke 12:15).

As believers we should be able to control our desires through living wisely. Ungodly desires are hostile to God.

What The Bible Says?

Psalm 37:16

Better the little that the righteous have than the wealth of many wicked.

Proverbs 15:16

Better a little with the fear of the LORD than great wealth with turmoil.

1 Timothy 6:6, 8

But godliness with contentment is great gain. But if we have food and clothing, we will be content with that.

Proverbs 30:8-9

Keep falsehood and lies far from me; give me neither poverty nor riches, but give me only my daily bread. Otherwise, I may have too much and disown you and say, "Who is the LORD?" or I may become poor and steal, and so dishonour the name of my God.

Matthew 6:11, 25

Give us today our daily bread. Therefore I tell you, do not worry about your life, what you will eat or drink or about your body, what you will wear. Is not life more important than food, and the body more important than clothes?

Luke 22:35

Then Jesus asked them, "When I sent you without purse, bag or sandals, did you lack anything?" Nothing, they answered.

Hebrews 13:5

Keep your lives free from the love of money and be content with what you have, because God has said, "Never will I leave you; never will I forsake you".

Chapter 9

WHAT DOES THE WORD CHRISTIAN MEAN?

The word Christian is derived from the Greek word 'Christos' for 'Messiah' which in Hebrew means 'Anointed One'. In the Old Testament, kings, prophets and priests were anointed with oil to consecrate or get them ready for their specific duties. The 'ian' attached at the end of the name Christ changes the name to Christian which means one who belongs to Christ or a follower of Christ, and it is mentioned in the Bible (New Testament) three times (Acts 11:26; 26:28; 1 Peter 4:16). The disciples were first called Christians in Antioch during Paul's early ministry work (Acts 11:26). Christians go through trials because of their belief in Jesus and such trials are regarded as participating in the suffering of Christ. 1 Peter 4:16 encourages us that "If you suffer as a Christian, do not be ashamed but praise God that you bear the name".

Christianity is about transformation and change. When a person hears the gospel (the good news) and believes in Jesus Christ and he is baptised in the name of the Father and of the Son and of the Holy Spirit (Matt. 28:19), he is saved (Mark 16:16) and belongs to Christ (Christian). A Christian goes through a transformation process which gives him a new life, a new heart and a new self (Eph. 4:22-24). If we belong to Christ (Christians) people must see changes in our lives (2 Cor. 5:17). In Romans 12:1-2, Apostle Paul tells us that this transformation involves renewal of our minds, and he goes further in Phil. 2:5-8, stating that the renewal is about having a new mindset or attitude that you find in Christ himself. In other words a Christian should start growing in Christlikeness in the way of his thinking and living. Jesus showed the humble nature of his mission and ministry by his obedience to death, even death on the cross, to pay for our sins (Phil. 2:8). Jesus asked his followers (Christians) to take up the cross and follow his example of selfless sacrifice (Matt. 16:24). His cross is a symbol of his love, obedience and selflessness, which he passed on to us. Jesus did not tell the disciples to carry the cross and follow him once a year or once a month or once a week or every Sunday but every moment in our lives, we must carry the cross.

The Church and its Impact on the Christian

The church is where God's people (Christians) are prepared for the ministry of Jesus, so that the body of Christ may be built up. The church is equipped with workers of varying talents (Eph. 4:11-13) to transform those who belong to the body of Christ (Christians) into new life (Christlikeness). As Christians we are all in the ministry of Jesus. The change in our lives (new heart, new mind, and new self) should be reciprocated in our communities, workplace, political life, social life, sporting life, schools, universities, occupations, vocations, just to mention a few. 2 Corinthians 5:17 says, "If anyone is in Christ, he is a new creation; the old has gone, the new has come". Every Christian is expected to be a member of a church that believes in Jesus as our Lord and saviour and doing what he asked them to do (1 Cor. 12:2-27). Unfortunately some Christians have ended up only going to church. Jesus Christ did not shed his blood on the cross to pay for our sins, only for us to end up going to church. The church will not change you unless you are hearing something and understanding and doing it. Start with milk and grow into solid food (Eph. 4:11-14).

Christ wants us to take our new life, new heart, new mind and new self to the world so that we can save souls for him. Titus 2:14 says, "Who gave himself for us to redeem us from all wickedness and purify for himself a people that are his very own, eager to do what is good". Going to church is necessary for every Christian but that is not a guarantee that you are a Christian because even the devil goes to church. What you believe, what you obey and the fruit you bear are what matter and the fruit is love, joy, peace, patience, kindness, goodness, faithfulness and self-control (Gal. 5:22-23). Through these qualities, people around you can come to accept Jesus. Nicodemus believed in Jesus but he did not obey him. Luke 11:28 says, "Blessed rather are those who hear the word of God and obey it". 1 John 2:5 says, "But if anyone obeys his word, God's love is truly made complete in him. This is how we know we are in him". Matthew 7:21 says, "Not everyone who says to me, Lord, Lord, will enter the kingdom of Heaven, but only he who does the will of my Father who is in Heaven". The parable of the Good Samaritan (Luke 10:25-37) shows us that it was the non-believer, the pagan Samaritan who showed mercy, love and kindness to the afflicted while the Levi, and the Priest did nothing to help the afflicted. They believed that their religious activities in the temple and church were all that mattered.

As Christians, we have been commanded to carry the gospel (good news) which has impacted and changed our lives to those around us. As Christians our examples are important. You should not expect those around you to accept your doctrine and ignore your personal examples. Jesus passed the baton to the twelve disciples. The baton is the good news (the gospel) and we have it in our hands (new life). There are people who will go to hell because we have failed. A chain is only strong at its weakest point. The weakest point in the church may be you in spreading the gospel through your new life. Your personal examples are what will win souls for Jesus.

What Does the Bible Say?

Ephesians 4:22-24

You were taught, with regard to your former way of life, to put off your old self, which is being corrupted by its deceitful desires; to be made new in the attitude of your minds; and to put on the new self, created to be like God in true righteousness and holiness.

1 Peter 2:24

He himself bore our sins in his body on the tree, so that we might die to sins and live for righteousness; by his wounds, you have been healed.

Romans 6:4, 6

We were therefore buried with him through baptism into death in order that, just as Christ was raised from the dead through the glory of the Father, we too may live a new life. For we know that our old self was crucified with him so that the body ruled by sin might be done away with, that we should no longer be slaves to sin.

Galatians 2:20

I have been crucified with Christ and I no longer live but Christ lives in me. The life I live in the body, I live by faith in the son of God, who loved me and gave himself for me.

1 John 2:6

Whoever claims to live in him must walk as Jesus did.

Chapter 10

HOW DO WE KNOW JESUS CHRIST IS GOD?

---- ❋ ----

Jesus Christ is God. He deserves our praise and worship. John 1:1 says, "In the beginning was the Word, and the Word was with God and the Word was God". Jesus Christ is fully God and fully man. He is one with God as he says in John 10:30, "I and my Father are one". Christ is the exact picture of God (John 12:44-45). He is the second person of the Trinity. Jesus is the model of God's character: All the fullness of the deity is in him (Col. 2:9). He demonstrated his love to all people (Mark 10:21). He demonstrated sacrificial love and faithfulness when he paid for our sins with his blood shed on the cross to make us justified before God (1 John 3:16). In John 10:15,18 Christ said, "Just as the Father knows me and I know the Father, and I lay down my life for the sheep. No one takes it from me, but I lay it down of my own accord. I have authority to lay it down and authority to take it up". His Holiness due to his sinlessness made him a perfect sacrificial lamb to die for the sins of the world. Jesus was compassionate and showed mercy throughout his ministry to those in need (Matt. 9:36). Jesus is faithful. His promises to supply our needs and protect us never fail (John 6:32-35; Luke 22:35). Jesus is the only sinless person who has ever lived on Earth (Heb. 7:26). John 1:18 says, "No one has ever seen God, but God the one and only son, who is at the Father's side has made him known".

Some Other Bible Passages Which Show That Jesus is God

Jesus fulfilled the prophecy of Isaiah "Immanuel, God with us" (Isa. 7:14; Matt. 1:23). In the book of Isaiah 9:6 it says, "For unto us a child is born, and he will be called Wonderful Counsellor, Mighty God, Everlasting Father, Prince of Peace". Thomas confesses in John 20:28 that Jesus is God when he says, "My Lord and my God". Hebrews 1:3 says, "Jesus is the radiance of God's glory and the exact representation of his being". Colossians 1:15-16 says, "Jesus is the image of the invisible God, the first born over all creation and the one by whom all things were created". Colossians 1:19 says, "God was pleased to have all his fullness dwell in him".

Jesus Christ is our great God and Saviour (**Titus 2:13**).

Who being in very nature God did not consider equality with God (**Philippians 2:6**).

Then God said, "Let us make man in our image, in our likeness" (**Genesis 1:26**).

"Each of the four living creatures had six wings and was covered with eyes all round and even under his wings. Day and night they never stop saying: Holy, holy, holy is the Lord God Almighty who was, and is, and is to come" (**Revelation 4:8**).

Jesus is God who came in human flesh. Believing in God is also believing in Jesus (**John 9:38; 20:28**). He is worthy of our praise and worship.

Chapter 11

DO YOU LOVE GOD?

The Two Greatest Commandments Are:

The first is, "You must love the Lord your God with all your heart and with all your soul and with all your mind and with all your strength" (Mark 12:30). The second commandment is love your neighbour as you love yourself (Mark 12:31). John 15:13 says, "Greater love has no one than this; that he lay down his life for his friends". God created us in his likeness and wants us to reciprocate his love back to him in a relationship of mutual love. Precisely, loving God is by obeying his commandments. In Romans 12:1, Paul tells believers to emulate our saviour Jesus Christ by offering themselves as living sacrifices devoted to God. God's disposition about sin is not different from the Old Testament. In the New Testament he still considers those who are sinful and unrighteous as his enemies (Rom. 5:10; Col. 1:21). If you love God, sin should no longer hold dominion on you. For example, if you love God, you will not steal or tell lies; in fact you will say no to unforgiveness, corruption, idolatry, adultery, envy, cheating, hatred, greed, wickedness and so on. Those who belong to Christ Jesus have crucified the sinful nature with its passions and desires (Gal. 5:24). Everyone who confesses the name of the Lord must turn away from wickedness (2 Tim. 2:19).

How Do You Know You Love God?

If you truly love God, then you will keep his commandments. In John 14:23-24 Jesus says, "If anyone loves me, he will obey my teaching. He who does not love me will not obey my teaching. These words you hear, are not my own; they belong to the Father who sent me." 1 John 4:20 also tells us: if anyone says "I love God" yet hates his brother, he is a liar. For anyone who does not love his brother, whom he has seen, cannot love God whom he has not seen. The second commandment is love your neighbour as yourself. If you love others sacrificially, it is God you love.

Sacrificial Love

Jesus talks about sacrificial love. Love one another as I have loved you. Be imitators of God. Selfless love is you first before me. Genuine love demands self-denial. John 15:12 says, *"My command is this: love each other as I have loved you"*. Love others the way you love yourselves. God is love. Do nothing out of selfish ambition, or vain conceit, but in humility consider others better than yourselves. Each one of you should look not only to your own interests but also to the interests of others. God says, love your enemies also. If you love God, then you will have the ability to love others including your enemies. *Rejoice with those who rejoice and mourn with those who mourn* (Rom. 12:15).

Our Lord Jesus modeled genuine love by saving us from our sins (Mark 10:42-45). His love should motivate us and help us to practice sacrificial love towards others (Matt. 22:39; John 3:16). It should prompt us to practice self-control, longsuffering with others and forgiveness towards those who wrong us. It will make us to repay evil with good (Rom. 12:14). Our love for the truth should be a motivation to us to act in the best interest of others (1 Cor.13:4-8) in the hope that they may be restored to God (2 Tim. 2:24-26).

Brotherly Love

Brotherly love is a significant component of the second commandment, "Love your neighbour as yourself". This love is mostly directed to believers to love themselves. It is agape love which is a Christian love. Galatians 6:10 says "Therefore, as we have opportunity, let us also do good to all people, especially to those who belong to the family of believers. Hebrews 13:1 says,

"Keep on loving each other as brothers". Brotherly love therefore involves a life of faith whereby we learn to show our love for God by attending to the needs of fellow believers whom God brings into their lives. Apostle Paul in Galatians 6:10 says, "Therefore, as we have opportunity let us do good to all people, especially to those who belong to the family of believers". Paul instructs the church at Rome to love one another with brotherly affection (Rom. 12:10) as part of the Christian life. In 1 Thessalonians 4:9-10, this is what Paul says, "Now about brotherly love, we do not need to write to you, for you yourselves have been taught by God to love each other. And in fact, you do love all the brothers throughout Macedonia. Yet we urge you brothers to do so more and more." Paul thus recognizes the supernatural origin of this new love among believers. 1 Peter 1:22 says, "Now that you have purified yourselves by obeying the truth so that you have sincere love for your brothers, love one another deeply from the heart". Going to church does not mean that you love God. The devil also goes to church. If you love God, you will obey his commandments. If you love others, it is God you are loving. If you love God, you will have the ability to love others including your enemies.

The Word of Spirit and of Power

Proverbs 21:3

To do what is right and just is more acceptable to the Lord than sacrifice.

1 Samuel 15:22

Does the Lord delight in burnt offerings and sacrifices as much as in obeying the voice of the LORD? To obey is better than sacrifice and to heed is better than the fat of rams.

Micah 6:8

He has showed you, O man, what is good. And what does the LORD require of you? To act justly and to love mercy and to walk humbly with your God.

Mark 12:33

To love him with all your heart, with all your understanding and with all your strength, and to love your neighbor as yourself is more important than all your burnt offerings and sacrifices.

John 3:16

For God so loved the world that he gave his one and only son, that whoever believes in him, shall not perish but have eternal life.

Romans 12:1

Therefore, I urge you, brothers, in view of God's mercy, to offer your bodies as living sacrifices, holy and pleasing to God – this is your spiritual act of worship.

Philippians 2:3-4

Do nothing out of selfish ambition or vain conceit, but in humility consider others better than yourselves. Each of you should look not only to your own interests, but also to the interests of others.

John 15:10

If you obey my commands, you will remain in my love just as I have obeyed my Father's commands and remain in his love.

John 15:12-14

My command is this: Love each other as I have loved you. Greater love has no one than this, that he lay down his life for his friends. You are my friend if you do what I command.

1 Peter 4:8

Above all, love each other deeply because love covers over a multitude of sins.

John 13:34

A new command I give you: Love one another. As I have loved you, so you must love one another.

Ephesians 5:2

And I live a life of love, just as Christ loved us and gave himself up for us as a fragrant offering and sacrifice to God.

Proverbs 10:12

Hatred stirs up dissension, but love covers over all wrongs.

Luke 6:35

But love your enemies, do good to them and lend to them without expecting to get anything back. Then your reward will be great and you will be sons of the Most High because he is kind to the ungrateful and wicked.

Proverbs 24:17

Do not gloat when your enemy falls; when he stumbles, do not let your heart rejoice.

1 Peter 3:9

Do not repay evil with evil or insult with insult, but with blessing, because to this you were called so that you may inherit a blessing.

1 John 3:18

Dear children, let us not love with words or tongue but with actions and in truth.

Ephesians 4:32

Be kind and compassionate to one another, forgiving each other, just as in Christ God forgave you.

Jude 21

Keep yourselves in God's love as you wait for the mercy of our Lord Jesus Christ to bring you to eternal life.

John 15:8-10

This is to my Father's glory, that you bear much fruit, showing yourselves to be my disciples. As the Father has loved me, so have I loved you. Now remain in my love. If you obey my commands,

*you will remain in my love, just as I have obeyed my Father's
commands and remain in his love.*

Romans 5:8

*But God demonstrates his own love for us in this; while we were
still sinners, Christ died for us.*

1 John 4:16

*And so we know and rely on the love God has for us. God is love.
Whoever lives in love lives in God and God in him.*

John 15:12

My command is this: love each other as I have loved you.

1 John 2:5

*But if anyone obeys his word, God's love is truly made complete
in him. This is how we know we are in him.*

Galatians 5:22-23

*But the fruit of the Spirit is love, joy, peace, patience, kindness,
goodness, faithfulness, gentleness and self-control*

Deuteronomy 27:10

*Obey the LORD your God and follow his commands and decrees
that I give you today.*

Matthew 5:44-45

*But I tell you: love your enemy and pray for those who persecute
you, that you may be sons of your Father in heaven. He causes his
sun to rise on the evil and the good, and sends rain on the
righteous and the unrighteous.*

1 Corinthians 13:4-7

*Love is patient, love is kind. It does not envy, it does not boast, it
is not proud. It is not rude, it is not self-seeking, it is not easily
angered, it keeps no record of wrongs. Love does not delight in
evil but rejoices with the truth. It always protects, always trusts,
always hopes, always perseveres.*

Chapter 12

WHY DO WE FEAR GOD?

— ❋ —

The Bible makes it clear that "The fear of the LORD is the beginning of knowledge (Prov. 1:7) and the beginning of wisdom" (Prov. 9:10). Apart from the fear of God, other fears are wrong. Christ also made it clear to believers to only fear God "I tell you, my friends, do not be afraid of those who kill the body and after that can do no more, but I will show you whom you should fear. Fear him who, after the killing of the body has power to throw you into hell. Yes, I tell you fear him" (Luke 12:4-5).

Every aspect of the life of believers is expected to be conducted under the direction of God and without the fear of God, it becomes impossible for believers to live a life pleasing to God. In the book of Exodus 20:18-20, when the people saw the thunder and lightning and heard the trumpet and saw the mountain in smoke, they trembled with fear. They stayed at a distance and said to Moses, "Speak to us yourself and we will listen. But do not have God speak to us or we will die. Moses said to the people, do not be afraid. God has come to test you, so that the fear of God will be with you to keep you from sinning".

The fear of God is not said in the sense of terror but of reverence. To fear God is one of the standard biblical descriptions for being a follower of God (Acts 10:2). The fear of God is another way of expressing how someone is in genuine relationship with God. For the ungodly or even the unrepentant believer, the Bible makes it clear that there is fear in the sense of terror or panic in the end times as God will judge the world (Heb. 10:27,31).

The Bible never records a personal encounter with God, without being visibly shaken by God's awesomeness. In God's presence, Moses hides his face (Exod. 3:6).

What Does the Fear of God Look Like?

Having a genuine fear of God is simply one way of describing how a believer is in a genuine relationship with God.

For a believer, the fear of the LORD is a respectful reverence to the awesomeness of God's glory, his holiness and majesty which leads to a godly life. The positive aspect of fear involves a positive seeking of God and a new desire to please him, and not to displease him. This is the purifying aspect of the fear of the Lord and is reflected in Proverbs 16:6: "Through the fear of the LORD, a man avoids evil". It is a deep understanding and appreciation that God is our creator, our sustainer, our saviour and He owns the whole world.

A believer should have confidence in God's love and the sufficiency of Christ's sacrifice on the cross for the atonement of sin which defeats such negative fear, rendering it out of place.

In his pride the wicked does not seek God; in all his thoughts there is no room for God (Ps 10:4). This is opposite of those who fear God. They regularly meditate upon God, reflecting on him, looking for his help and sustenance, seeking for his direction in making life decisions, actively seeking to please him and obey him in everything they do. Fearing God means that we trust him more than we trust ourselves or anyone else.

God's Awesomeness

God's awesomeness should not invite fear in the sense of terror but reverence to him – "God the blessed and only Ruler, the King of Kings and Lord of Lords, who alone is immortal who lives in unapproachable light; whom no one has seen or can see. To him be honour and might for ever.. Amen" (1 Tim. 6: 15-16). "I am the Alpha and Omega" says the Lord God "who is and who was and who is to come, the Almighty" (Rev. 1:8).

The Word of Spirit and of Power

Psalm 103:1 – 2

Praise the Lord, O my soul; all my inmost being, praise his holy name. Praise the Lord, O my soul, and forget not all his benefits.

Psalm 145:10

All you have made will praise you, O Lord; your saints will extol you.

Psalm 145:2

Every day I will praise you and extol your name forever and ever.

Revelation 4:11

You are worthy, our Lord and God, to receive glory and honour and power for you created all things, and by your will they were created and have their being.

Psalm 63:3 -5

Because your love is better than life, my lips will glorify you. I will praise you as long as I live and in your name I will lift up my hands. My soul will be satisfied as with the richest of foods; with singing lips my mouth will praise you.

Psalm 31:1

In you O Lord, I have taken refuge; let me never be put to shame; deliver me in your righteousness.

Luke 1:46 – 47

And Mary said: "My soul glorifies the Lord and my spirit rejoices in God my savior".

2 Corinthians 1:3

Praise be to the God and Father of our Lord Jesus Christ, the Father of compassion and the God of all comfort.

Chapter 13

HOW GOD SPEAKS TO US

1. In the Old Testament God Spoke Directly to the People and Through the Prophets

In the Old Testament times, God speaks directly to people through the Prophets in various ways (Heb. 1:1). God also spoke to individuals and directly to the people themselves. For example, God spoke to the assembly of Israel at Mount Sinai when they were given the Ten Commandments (Deut. 5:4-27). God spoke to Moses from a burning bush (Exod. 3:1-10); God spoke to Abraham to leave his country and his people to a land he would show him (Gen. 12:1). God also spoke to Abraham to offer his son Isaac as a burnt offering (Gen. 22:2). After the death of Moses, God spoke to Joshua promising to be with him as he was with Moses. He commanded Joshua to meditate and obey everything that is written in the law (Josh. 1:8). Not every Prophet's testimony was believed in the Old Testament. God used miracles to support his message. In Exodus 4:29-31, Moses and Aaron brought together all the elders of Israelites, and Aaron told them everything that the LORD had said to Moses. He performed signs before the people, and they believed. And when they heard that the LORD was concerned about them and had seen their misery, they bowed down and worshipped. After the death of Moses, God spoke through Prophets.

2. In the New Testament God Spoke Through Jesus Christ and His Disciples

In the New Testament before the public ministry of Jesus, John the Baptist prepared the way for him by preaching baptism of repentance to the people. Luke 3:3-4 says, "He went into all the country around Jordan, preaching a baptism of repentance for the forgiveness of sins. As it is written in the book of the words of Isaiah the prophet". The public ministry of Jesus and His miracles were performed among the people. Sometimes he also sent out the disciples to preach and perform miracles (Matt. 10:1-10). After his resurrection and ascension, the followers of Jesus started proclaiming the "good news" (gospel) of what Jesus did and calling on the people to "Repent and be baptised, every one of you, in the name of Jesus Christ for the forgiveness of your sins" (Acts 2:38). The New Testament account of God is given through Jesus Christ, the son of God and his disciples (Heb. 1:2).

3. The Bible is the Word of God: In the Present Age God Speaks to Us Through the Bible.

What is written in the Bible, both in the Old Testament and New Testament carry the same authority as the spoken word of God. The Bible is the word of God in a written text revealed and breathed by God (2 Tim 3:16-17). God is the ultimate author of the Bible. Because the Bible is the divinely inspired word of God reliably composed in the originals without error, it is binding upon people in their relationship with their God as well as their relationship with their fellow human beings. The word is the special revelation of God to humans, specifically the truth communicated from God to his human creatures by supernatural intervention, including disclosure of his mind and will, his attributes and his redemptive plans. This revealed word is inspired. Inspiration is an act of the Holy Spirit of God.

Free from Error

The word of God is free from error in every matter addressed, and infallible, true in every matter addressed. The locus of inspiration and infallibility is in the original manuscripts and not the translations. A translation is reliable when it accurately reflects the meaning of the inspired originals (2 Peter 1:21).

The word of God is true and trustworthy and thus a reliable rule of faith and conduct. Despite the fact that the Bible was written over eleven hundred years ago, time, culture and distance should not have any material effect on the word except the language due to a variety of interpretations arising from community use of biblical text. It is the revealed word of God, the contents of which were progressively made known to authors guided by the Holy Spirit. In the beginning was the Word and the Word was with God and the Word was God (John 1:1).

Trustworthy

The Bible is true, trustworthy and without a doubt is a reliable rule of conduct and discipline for believers. 2 Timothy 3:16-17 says, "All scripture is God breathed and is useful for teaching, rebuking, correcting and training in righteousness, so that the man of God may be thoroughly equipped for every good work". When God says something, he upholds his name and his word. His creation is perfect. Anything created works in uniform. The moon does not clash with the sun (Eccl. 1:5). There is no conflict in his creation (Gen 1:1-31). When he says I will provide for your needs, it is settled. When he says I will never leave you alone, it is settled. The Bible is a complete living book for faith and conduct. Anything you need for living is there. Anything you need for your marriage is in the Bible. Anything you need for your children is in the Bible. Anything you need for your financial life is in the Bible.

The Word is Jesus Christ

The word of God is the eternal Lord Jesus Christ (John 1:1; 1John 1:1-4) who came in flesh and blood so that we might seek the glory of the eternal God. Jesus Christ as the word of God gives us our lives (John 1:4; 10:10) sustains our lives (John 5:24) and ultimately renders just judgment regarding our lives (John 5:30).

The Bible is an authoritative proclamation from God to us that must be obeyed; that must be sought, that cannot be ignored. When we are reading the Bible or listening to the reading of the

Bible by a preacher or pastor, it should be perceived as listening to God. What is written in the Bible is the Word of God (2 Chron. 34:21; John 1:1). When we read it or listen to its reading, we are listening to the Word of God. The prophecies in the Old Testament point to Jesus and he is at the heart of the gospel (Eph. 1:10). Because of the infiltration of the ministry by false prophets, teachers and evangelists, we must be careful in accepting what we hear. Pass what you hear through quality control. Refer to the Bible to make sure that what you hear is in line with what the Bible says and also in line with what you believe.

Before we commence reading or studying the Bible, we should ask God in prayer to open our blind eyes, so that we can see wonderful things (Ps. 119:18). In Luke 24:45, Jesus opened the minds of his disciples so that they could understand the scriptures. We must always remember that the Bible is not a book we can sideline for a while. Make it a duty to set aside time to read the Bible daily. Avoid the temptation of reading the Bible randomly. If you are listening to the preaching of the Old Testament or the New Testament, they are the words of God that you are hearing. Hebrews 4:12 says, "The word of God is living and active. Sharper than any double-edged sword, it penetrates even to dividing soul and spirit, joints and marrow; it judges the thoughts and attitudes of the heart".

The Bible is one of the greatest resources that believers have but unfortunately it has been under-utilised. Spend time with God by reading the Bible daily. Pray always that God will help you grow in the knowledge of the word and also help you read the Bible from the beginning to the end. It is through reading the Bible that you know God. When you know God, you will constantly be under His compass.

Psalm 119 and the Word

Psalm 119 tells us that God pierced the darkness of our existence with the light of his Word to make himself known to us. It is his Word spoken to us and preserved for us. The Psalmist also teaches us that the Word is the Word of God. When he pierced our darkness, he lit the part of freedom for us with his Word. He described himself, defined righteousness, declared his love, announced his promises and issued his warnings.

In Psalm 119, the Word is elaborately discussed. In Psalm 119, the Word is translated in the NIV as 'Words' (vs. 57) 'Commands' (vs. 60), 'Laws' (vs. 62), 'Precepts' (vs. 63) and 'Decrees' (vs. 64).

4. God Speaks to Us through the Holy Spirit in the Present Age

God also speaks to us through the Holy Spirit. When the spirit of truth comes, he will guide you into all truth. He will not speak on his own; he will speak only what he hears, and he will tell you what is yet to come. He will bring glory to me by taking from what is mine and making it known to you (John 16:13-15). The Holy Spirit is our spiritual compass which directs our consciences if we listen to Him. The Holy Spirit restrains us from sinful desires (Gal. 5:16-17). Those who receive the Holy Spirit will understand the Bible more deeply (1 Cor. 2:9-16). The Holy Spirit is God's presence in our midst (John 16:13-15). Believers share the same fellowship, the same spirit and the same Lord.

5. God Speaks to Us Through Tests and Trials

God speaks to us through circumstances. He gets our attention through restlessness when we encounter tests and trials which lead to constant and persistent prayers. No discipline seems pleasant at the time but painful. However, it produces a harvest of righteousness and peace for those who have been trained by it (Heb. 12:11-12). God is faithful. He will not let you be tempted beyond what you can bear. But when you are tempted, he will also provide a way out so that you can stand up under it (1 Cor. 10:13). During trials you need to be patient and wait rightly by exercising our spiritual amoury through persistent prayers for the Lord's deliverance. It is when we are passing through our trial times that God starts to teach us about himself which leads to deep and clearer knowledge of him.

The Word of Spirit and of Power

Matthew 5:18

I tell you the truth, until heaven and earth disappear, not the smallest letter, not the least stroke of a pen will by any means disappear from the law until everything is accomplished.

John 1:1

In the beginning was the Word, and the Word was with God, and the Word was God.

John 17:17

Sanctify them by the truth; your word is truth.

1 John 1:1-4

That which was from the beginning, which we have heard, which we have seen with our eyes, which we have looked at and our hands have touched – this we proclaim concerning the Word of life. The life appeared; we have seen it and testify to it, and we proclaim to you the eternal life, which was with the father and has appeared to us. We proclaim to you what we have seen and heard, so that you also may have fellowship with us. And our fellowship is with the Father and with his son, Jesus Christ. We write this to make our joy complete.

2 Peter 1:21

For prophecy never had its origin in the will of man, but men spoke from God as they were carried along by the Holy Spirit.

Hebrews 4:12

For the word of God is living and active. Sharper than any double – edged sword, it penetrates even to dividing soul and spirit, joints and marrow, it judges the thoughts and attitudes of the heart.

Psalm 119:57

You are my portion, O LORD; I have promised to obey your words.

Psalm 119:60-64

I will hasten and not delay to obey your commands. Though the wicked bind me with ropes, I will not forget your law. At midnight I rise to give you thanks for your righteous laws. I am a friend to all who fear you, to all who follow your precepts. The earth is filled with your love, O LORD; teach me your decrees.

Romans 7:22

For in my inner being, I delight in God's law.

Psalm 119:97

Oh, how I love your law. I meditate on it all day long.

Jeremiah 15:16

When your words came, I ate them; they were my joy and my heart's delight, for I bear your name. O LORD God Almighty.

Job 23:12

I have not departed from the commands of his lips; I have treasured the words of his mouth more than my bread.

Psalm 40:8

I desire to do your will, O my God; your law is within my heart.

Psalm 19:8, 10

The precepts of the LORD are right, giving joy to the heart. The commands of the LORD are radiant, giving light to the eyes. They are more precious than gold, than much pure gold, they are sweeter than honey, than honey from the comb.

James 1:22-25

Do not merely listen to the word, and so deceive yourselves. Do what it says. Anyone who listens to the word but does not do what it says, is like a man who looks at his face in a mirror and after looking at himself, goes away and immediately forgets what he looks like. But the man who looks intently into the perfect law that gives freedom, and continues to do this, not forgetting what he has heard, but doing it, he will be blessed in what he does.

Psalm 19:7-8

The law of the LORD is perfect, reviving the soul. The statutes of the LORD are trustworthy, making wise the simple. The precepts of the LORD are right, giving joy to the heart. The commands of the LORD are radiant, giving light to the eyes.

2Timothy 3:16-17

All scripture is God-breathed and is used for teaching, rebuking, correcting and training in righteousness, so that the man of God may be thoroughly equipped for every good work.

Ezra 7:26

Whoever does not obey the law of your God and the law of the king must surely be punished by death, banishment, confiscation of property, or imprisonment.

1 Corinthians 2:13

This is what we speak, not in words taught us by human wisdom, but in words taught by the Spirit, expressing spiritual truths in spiritual words.

Chapter 14

MEDITATION

---------------------------------- ❀ ----------------------------------

Meditation in the Old Testament is primarily focusing on the will of God, verbally repeating God's commandments day and night (Ps 1:2). In Josh 1:8, God says to Joshua, "Do not let this Book of the law depart from your mouth; meditate on it day and night, so that you may be careful to do everything written in it. Then you will be prosperous and successful". To maintain focus in their meditation, Jewish men wore tassels. Jesus also wore tassels (Matt 9:20).

Meditation is one of the most important activities in the life of a believer of Jesus. Paul strongly encourages his readers to meditate upon Jesus' ministry and also to reflect upon the exalted Christ (Col 3:2). Meditation involves focusing on the Word of God, verbally repeating verses of the scripture. Meditation shows God is a personal God. He knows what you need and he is unlimited. If we confess our sins, he is faithful and just. Meditation increases our love for God. It is a concentration on God. My God will supply all my needs. Godly meditation strengthens our faith and increases our awareness of the presence of God, infusing in us joy. Meditation is good for our hearts. It shows that you and God are walking in harmony every moment.

Benefits of meditation:

- It quietens your spirit
- Enlightens our minds
- Increases our energy
- Purifies our heart

Distractions from godly meditations:

- Bitterness
- Anger
- Hatred
- Unforgiveness
- Hostility
- Resentment

Attitudes that affect godly meditation

- Unbelief is very destructive
- Holding a grudge
- Fear is distractive from godly meditation.

Psalm 19:14 says, "May the word of my mouth and the meditation of my heart be pleasing in your sight, O LORD, my Rock and my Redeemer".

The Word of Spirit and of Power

Deuteronomy 11:18

Fix these words of mine in your hearts and minds; tie them as symbols on your hands and bind them on your foreheads.

Joshua 1:8

Do not let this Book of the law depart from your mouth; meditate on it day and night, so that you may be careful to do everything written in it. Then you will be prosperous and successful.

Psalm 37:31

The law of his God is in his heart; his feet do not slip.

Psalm 119:11

I have hidden your word in my heart that I might not sin against you.

Psalm 17:4

As for the deeds of men - by the word of your lips I have kept myself from the ways of the violent.

2 Peter 1:19

And we have the word of the prophets made more certain, and you will do well to pay attention to it, as to a light shining in a dark place, until the day dawns and the morning star rises in your hearts.

Romans 15:4

For everything that was written in the past was written to teach us, so that through endurance and encouragement of the Scriptures we might have hope.

Chapter 15

WALKING IN THE HOLY SPIRIT

---- ✳ ----

Believers cannot serve God rightly without the presence of the Holy Spirit in their midst. The Holy Spirit is our comforter and counsellor (John 14:16). The Holy Spirit is the spirit of wisdom and of understanding; the Spirit of counsel and of power, the Spirit of knowledge and of fear of the LORD (Isa. 11:2). Believers are the beneficiaries of the work of the Holy Spirit of God made available to them through Christ. Because of the presence of the Holy Spirit in our midst, we are not alone because Christ's own Spirit is with us to lead and guide us (2 Cor. 3:16-17). The Holy Spirit teaches us the truth. He reminds us of the truth from the Word of God. He convicts us of our sins (John 16:8-13). He bears witness that we have been saved (Acts 1:8). The Holy Spirit is the spirit of adoption (Rom. 8:15), through which we become the children of God. We must be sensitive always to His promptings and guidance in our lives. If the spirit prompts us to do something, we should do it (Eph. 1:13). The Holy Spirit controls and guides our conscience. We cannot live a godly life without dependence on the leadership of the Holy Spirit in our lives because our conscience is controlled by the Holy Spirit (Rom. 9:1). Allow the spirit guide our conscience.

Human Conscience and the Holy Spirit

Human conscience is humanity's moral sense of right and wrong. It is an inborn awareness of wrong with an inclination towards thinking and acting rightly. In the Old Testament, moral awareness is described as a willingness to obey God's word (Deut. 30:14). The Holy Spirit guides our conscience distinguishing what is morally wrong or right. It restrains us from what is considered to be wrong. He directs our conscience by passing judgment within us. He directs our conscience for our protection if we listen to Him. Repentance and faith in Christ bring us back to God through godly living and make our conscience renewed and aligned with the new nature, which is Christ's nature (Rom. 12:1-2).

We live in a world that is becoming more and more ungodly due to pursuit of materialism and sin. Human conscience has also been affected in this new age. Human conscience can be divided into:

1. A Good Conscience

This is a conscience that is more informed and responds to the leadership of the Holy Spirit. A conscience where the word of God is living and active, penetrating the soul and spirit, and judging the thoughts and attitudes of the heart (Heb. 4:12). Furthermore, a conscience that is in alignment with the Holy Spirit lives in accordance with the spirit and the desires of the spirit (Rom. 8:5). A person with a good conscience is known as the spiritual man and makes judgments about all things (1 Cor. 2:15).

2. A Struggling Conscience

This is a conscience that is slow to respond to the Spirit. It is more on the side of the old nature. Christians that are not growing in the new nature and those that are weak in faith fall into this category. The old sinful nature struggles with the spirit led new nature. Both the old nature and new nature are in conflict (Gal. 5:17).

3. A Soiled Conscience

These are corrupted minds and corrupted consciences who claim to know God, but by their actions they deny him. They are detestable, disobedient and unfit for doing anything good (Titus

1:15-16). Although they know God, they never glorified him as God nor gave thanks to him; but their thinking became futile and their foolish hearts were darkened. Although they claimed to be wise, they become fools (Rom. 1:21-22). A conscience that does whatever it likes not considering whether it is right or wrong before God. It is no longer receptive to the leadership of the Holy Spirit. A conscience that is more on the side of wrong than of right.

4. A Seared Conscience

A seared conscience does not speak anymore. It does not listen to the Holy Spirit any longer. It is dead. It has become insensitive to the direction of the Holy Spirit because it is without the Holy Spirit and does not accept the things that come from the Spirit of God, for they are foolishness to him, and he cannot understand them, because they are spiritually discerned (1 Cor. 2:14). It is filled with every kind of wickedness, evil, greed and depravity. It is full of envy, murder, strife, deceit and malice. They are faithless, heartless and ruthless (Rom. 1:28-32).

When Can You Trust Your Conscience?

- When you have accepted the word of God.
- When you have a strong desire to obey God.
- When you prayerfully consider your decisions.
- When it sounds a warning in decision taking.
- When we feel guilty as soon as we take a wrong decision.

The Benefits of Walking in the Holy Spirit

A spirit-led conscience is there to protect us always. God is Spirit and his worshippers must worship in spirit and in truth (John 4:24). When the spirit of truth comes, he will guide you into all truth. He will not speak on his own; he will speak only what he hears, and he will tell you what is yet to come. He will bring glory to me by taking from what is mine and making it known to you (John 16:13-15). We are humans and we are limited. We only know what humans know. We can pray about what we know and not what we do not know. In fact we do not even have complete information about today. That is one of the reasons why the Holy Spirit intercedes for believers to cover the gap of what we do not know. Believers who are led by the Holy Spirit bear fruit known as the fruit of the spirit through their new nature in attitude and behaviour, which are pleasing to God and humanity. The fruit of the Spirit is love, joy, peace, patience, kindness, goodness, faithfulness, gentleness and self-control (Gal.5:22-23). My covid-19 experience is a glaring testimony of what the Holy Spirit does in the lives of believers. The Holy Spirit prompted me and prepared me for the covid-19 challenges.

Why Do We Pray in the Holy Spirit?

Christians are requested to pray in the Holy Spirit. Jude 20 says, "But you, dear friends build yourselves upon your most holy faith, and pray in the Holy Spirit". God is Spirit and his worshippers must worship him in spirit and in truth (John 4:24). God's Spirit is the spirit of prayer. Our weaknesses prevent us from relating rightly to God in prayer thus the Holy Spirit intercedes for us and pleads our case before God (Rom. 8:26-27). Christ is not physically present on Earth, hence he has promised to send the Holy Spirit to believers (John 16:7). We can only approach God through Christ with the help of the Holy Spirit. 1 John 5:14 says, "This is the confidence we have in approaching God; that if we ask anything according to his will, he hears us". The question is how do we know the will of God for us? The Holy Spirit knows the will of God for us and thus intercedes for us (Rom 8:26-27). We are also reminded to worship God not only in spirit but also in truth. Jesus calls the Holy Spirit the 'Spirit of Truth' (John 15:26) who will guide his followers in all truth speaking what he hears from the Father. John 16:12-15 says, "But when he, the Spirit of truth, comes he will guide you into all truth. He will not speak on his own; he will speak only what he hears, and he will tell you what is yet to come". Believers are therefore assured that the Holy Spirit knows their weakness and is praying side by side with them making up for their deficiencies and making their prayers what they ought to be before God. Believers receive the Holy Spirit by faith in Jesus Christ (Gal. 3:14) which makes them become beneficiaries of Christ's spiritual fullness.

The Word of Spirit and of Power

Titus 2:12

It teaches us to say "No" to ungodliness and worldly passions, and to live self-controlled, upright and godly lives in this present age.

Ephesians 4:12-13

To prepare God's people for works of service, so that the body of Christ may be built up until we all reach unity in the faith and in the knowledge of the son of God and become mature, attaining to the whole measure of the fullness of Christ.

Romans 8:6-7

The mind of sinful man is death, but the mind controlled by the Spirit is life and peace. The sinful mind is hostile to God. It does not submit to God's law, nor can it do so.

Galatians 5:22-23

But the fruit of the spirit is love, joy, peace, patience, kindness, goodness, faithfulness, gentleness and self-control.

John 16:13-14

But when he, the Spirit of truth, comes, he will guide you into all truth. He will not speak on his own; he will speak only what he hears, and he will tell you what is yet to come. He will bring glory to me by taking from what is mine and making it known to you.

John 14:26

But the Counsellor, the Holy Spirit, whom the Father will send in my name, will teach you all things and will remind you of everything I have said to you.

Isaiah 63:10

Yet they rebelled and grieved his Holy Spirit. So he turned and became their enemy and he himself fought against them.

1 Peter 2:5

You also, like living stones are being built into a spiritual house to be a holy priesthood, offering spiritual sacrifices acceptable to God through Jesus Christ.

1 Corinthians 3:16-17

Don't you know that you yourselves are God's temple and that God's Spirit lives in you? If anyone destroys God's temple, God will destroy him; for God's temple is sacred, and you are that temple.

1 Corinthians 6:19-20

Do you not know that your body is a temple of the Holy Spirit who is in you, whom you have received from God? You are not your own; you were bought at a price. Therefore honour God with your body.

Ephesians 2:21-22

In him the whole building is joined together and rises to become a holy temple in the Lord. And in him you too are being built together to become a dwelling in which God lives by his Spirit.

Romans 8:26

In the same way the spirit helps us in our weakness. We do not know what we ought to pray for, but the Spirit himself intercedes for us with groans that words cannot express.

Why Do We Pray in the Name of Jesus?

Firstly, Jesus wants believers to pray in His name and instructs them that prayer to God is to be made in His name. In John 14:13, Jesus says, "And I will do whatever you ask in my name, so that the son may bring glory to the Father". In John 15:16, Jesus says, "You did not choose me. But I chose you and appointed you to go and bear fruit, fruit that will last. Then the Father will give you whatever you ask in my name".

Secondly, God was pleased to have all His fullness dwell in him (Col. 1:19); He seated him at His right hand in the Heavenly realms, far above all rule and authority, power and dominion, and every title that can be given, not only in the present age, but also in the one to come (Eph. 1:20-21). The Father loves the son and has placed everything in his hands (John 3:35). God exalted him to the highest place and gave him the name that is above every name, that at the name of Jesus, every knee should bow, in heaven and on earth and under the earth, and every tongue confess that Jesus Christ is Lord, to the glory of God the Father (Phil. 2:9-11). For by him all things were created: things in heaven and on earth, visible and invisible, whether thrones or powers or rulers or authorities; all things were created by him and for him (Col. 1:16).

Thirdly, Praying in Jesus' name should not be taken as a mere routine. It is far more than that. Jesus is one with the Father (John 10:30). From the powers and authority given to Jesus by the Father he becomes the perfect mediator to intercede in our prayers. No nation, no king, no emperor comes first, only Jesus is Lord. He has all authority and power; only He deserves our praise and worship. Make it a duty to always have a moment by moment check on your relationship with Jesus. He signs off on our prayers to God. Make sure you are always connected to him in your daily walk with him and seek corrections when you are out of step through repentance. 1 John 1:9 says, "If we confess our sins, he is faithful and just and will forgive us our sins, and purify us from all unrighteousness". If you are not connected to him in your daily walk with him, do not expect your prayers to be approved. Jesus speaks to the Father in our defense (1 John 2:1).

Jesus ascended into Heaven and continues to intercede for us (Heb. 7:25). Our prayers are powerless if Christ does not intercede for us. Jesus' priesthood is forever and because he has experienced trials and sufferings on Earth, he is able to sympathise with us in our troubles (Heb. 4:15). Jesus Christ does not change. He is the same yesterday and today and forever (Heb. 13:8). In Heaven he becomes the perfect mediator between us and God, making his intercession for us more valid (Heb. 7:25). Believers are told to pray in spirit and truth and according to the will of God. How do we know the will of God if our prayers to God are not said in Jesus' name? How do we pray to God in spirit and truth if Jesus who is spirit and the truth does not intercede for us through our prayers to God in his name? Prayers to God said in Jesus' name are effective and powerful when the believer is connected to Jesus through genuine faith in him, his life and death. Without Christ interceding for us in prayers, God will not listen to our prayers. Praying in Jesus' name means we are connected to God through Christ who is our mediator. Christ is the author and perfecter of our faith. Prayer said in Jesus' name makes us always reflect on our relationship with Jesus. Are we in union with him? Are we living every moment rightly for Jesus? Praying in Jesus' name helps us reflect back on our walk with Jesus, ensuring that we are not out of step but in union with him.

The Word of the Spirit and Power

James 5:16

The prayer of a righteous man is powerful and effective.

1 John 1:6

If we claim to have fellowship with him, yet walk in darkness, we lie and do not live by the truth.

1 John 2:5

But if anyone obeys his word, God's love is truly made complete in him. This is how we know we are in him.

Luke 8:21

He replied, "My mother and brothers are those who hear God's word and put it into practice".

Galatians 6:9

Let us not become weary in doing good, for at the proper time we will reap a harvest if we do not give up.

James 5:11

As you know, we count as blessed those who have persevered.

James 4:4

The temptation to try to be friends with God and friends with the world at the same time is nothing less than spiritual adultery.

Hebrews 7:24-25

But Jesus lives forever, he has a permanent priesthood. Therefore he is able to save completely those who come to God through him because he always lives to intercede for them.

Chapter 16

WALKING IN FAITH TO BECOME FINISHERS

---- �֎ ----

In Hebrews 11:1 faith is defined as being sure of what we hope for and certain of what we do not see. Faith is belief in Jesus, hope in Jesus, trust in Jesus and reliance on Jesus. Faith is foremost the locus of trust and belief in the person of Jesus Christ. In the New Testament, Christ is the object of faith. Christ dwells in the hearts of believers through faith (Eph. 3:17). Christians live by faith (2 Cor. 5:7). In Ephesians 6:16, believers are advised to take up the shield of faith, with which you can extinguish all the flaming arrows of the evil one. Faith is at the core of Christianity and the Christian journey. It is the source of every believer's strength and comfort in times of extreme hardship. In Jesus' healing ministry, the faith of the one in need of healing has been central in his miraculous healing. Faith is instrumental to salvation as confirmed in Ephesians 2:8 which says, "For it is by grace you have been saved, through faith, and this not from yourselves, it is the gift of God". To possess faith, one must be loyal to God and to the gospel of Jesus Christ not minding all obstacles.

Faith Differs in Individual Believers

Faith in individual believer differs in its strength of conviction (Rom. 15:1). This could be due to the different levels of maturity. As believers grow in maturity, so also their faith grows (2 Cor. 10:15). They start with milk and go on to solid food. Some believers are weak in faith (Rom. 14:1), while others are strong in faith (Rom. 4:20-22). Genuine faith does not pretend. Little faith panics. If you have little faith you will panic. For example when Peter took his eyes off Jesus he started to panic (Matt. 14:28-31). Faith without works is dead (James 2:26). In John 6:28-29, belief (faith) is something that God requires of believers. Growing in faith requires growing in the knowledge of God through listening to the preaching of the Bible, reading and studying the Bible. The knowledge of God leads to action (works). Faith that is struggling always says, 'I want to read the Bible but the Bible is never read. I believe everything in the Bible, but never read the Bible'.

Faith and Works

Believe is a matter of the heart. Out of the heart proceeds the issues of life, actions of life. If you really believe in your heart, then it will really lead to action. Genuine faith shows the evidence of good works. Genuine works naturally accompany genuine faith. In Ephesians 2:8-10, works are described as the fruit of faith resulting from believing, "For it is by grace you have been saved, through faith and this is not from yourselves, it is the gift of God, not by works, so that no one can boast. For we are God's workmanship, created in Christ Jesus to do good works, which God prepared in advance for us to do". Faith without works is dead, as confirmed in James 2:26, "As the body without the spirit is dead, so faith without deeds is dead".

Works are regarded as doing the will of God. The will of God can mean performing deeds that are pleasing to God. In Colossians 1:10 it says, "And we pray this in order that you may live a life worthy of the Lord and may please him in every way; bearing fruit in every good work, growing in the knowledge of God". Righteous living is part of performing the deeds that are pleasing to God. Works also mean generosity, giving to charity, giving to people in need and showing kindness, love, mercy, compassion, justice to people. In Matthew 25:40, Christ says, "I tell you the truth, whatever you did for one of the least of these brothers of mine, you did for me". Faith and action work together, and faith is made complete by deed (James 2:22).

Can Good Works Please God?

Faith is a prerequisite for truly good works. God rewards out of his mercy and not out of human works (Rom. 9:16; Titus 3:5). Works that are not done in faith, even if they are acceptable or commended as good by human standards, are not acceptable to God because no one is righteous. All mankind is under sin (Rom. 3:9-8). In John 6:28-29, Jesus was asked "What must we do to do the works God requires?" Jesus answered, "The work of God is this: to believe in the one he has sent". Hebrews 11:6 says, "Without faith it is impossible to please God, because anyone who comes to him must believe that he exists and that he rewards those who earnestly seek him. Faith is foremost in the Christian journey to become finishers. It is the source of strength and comfort in times of extreme hardship. Faith is like an electrical cord that carries the power from the source to the appliance. God has unlimited power but to tap into that power, we need a cord and that is faith.

Can Good Works Save?

Ephesians 2:8-9 states that, "For it is by grace you have been saved, through faith and this not from yourselves, it is the gift of God, not by works, so that no one can boast". Salvation is a gift to be received by faith. Works therefore cannot save. Good works flow from faith. 1 Thessalonians 1:3 says, "We continually remember before our God and Father your work produced by faith, your labour prompted by love, and your endurance inspired by hope in our Lord Jesus Christ".

In Apostle Paul's letter to the Romans 2:6 says, "God will give each person according to what he has done". 2 Corinthians 5:10 says, "For we must all appear before the judgment seat of Christ, that each one may receive what is due to him for the things done while in the body, whether good or bad. The one who sows to please the spirit, from the spirit will reap eternal life" (Gal. 6:8). Faith provokes good works. In making one's calling and election sure, 2 Peter 1:5-8 says, "For this very reason, make every effort to add to your faith goodness; and to goodness, knowledge; and to knowledge, self-control; and to self-control, perseverance; and to perseverance, godliness; and to godliness, brotherly kindness; and to brotherly kindness, love. For if you possess these qualities in increasing measure, they will keep you from being ineffective and unproductive in your knowledge of our Lord Jesus Christ". Without faith it is impossible to please God, because anyone who comes to him must believe that he exists and that he rewards those who earnestly seek him (Heb. 11:6).

Faith and Redemption

Shedding blood and purchasing redemption is what Jesus did for us. There is power in the blood of Jesus. Because of the blood of Jesus we are sons and children of the living God. Without the shedding of blood there is no redemption of sins (Heb. 9:22). Help us Lord to remember and believe in the power of the blood. Under the new agreement (new covenant) Jesus has already done the work. In the old agreement (old covenant), it is all work. You have to do the work (Heb. 8:8-13). Faith in Jesus is what we need to enjoy the fruit of redemption.

Faith in Action

Abraham's life is described as a model of faith in the Bible. He is used as an example of faith in the scripture (Gal. 3:6-9). God chose Abraham and promised him that his descendants would become a great nation if they obeyed his commandments. Abraham trusted God's faithfulness to fulfill his promise and it was credited to him as righteousness. Abram lived a life of obedience to God and this is well acknowledged by the early church (Heb. 11:8-11, 17-19). These examples of faith in action credited to Abraham include firstly his departure from his homeland to a foreign land (Gen 12:1) when God commanded him to do so. Genesis 12:4 says. "So Abraham left, as the LORD had told him; and Lot went with him. Abraham was seventy-five years old when he set out from Haran". Abram left for the journey without any knowledge of the destination. He was elderly and childless when he took off on the journey. Hebrews 11:8 says, "By faith, Abraham, when called to go to a place he would later receive as his inheritance, obeyed and went, even though he did not know where he was going".

The second best known example of faith in action credited to Abraham, is the birth of his son, Isaac. Abraham trusted that God could raise an offspring for him despite the fact that he was about a hundred years old and that his body was as good as dead and Sarah's womb was also dead (Rom. 4:19-20). Despite all these setbacks, he did not waver through unbelief regarding the promise of God; instead he was strengthened in his faith and gave glory to God.

The third best known example of faith in action credited to Abraham is the offering of Isaac as a sacrifice. This is the greatest example of faith in action when he was commanded to offer Isaac his son as a burnt offering (Gen. 22:2). Abraham was commended for fearing God (Gen. 22:12). He is one of the heroes of faith in the Bible.

Christ's Resurrection and the Christian Faith

Christ resurrection is an event on which the foundation of the Christian faith is built. If Christ did not rise up from the dead, the Christian faith would have been futile. Resurrection is a major event to Christians as explained in Apostle Paul's letter in 1 Corinthians 15:17-19 which says, "And if Christ has not been raised, your faith is futile; you are still in your sins. Then those also who have fallen asleep in Christ are lost. If only for this life we have hope in Christ, we are to be pitied more than all men". Paul is inferring that if Christ was not raised from death, the Christian faith would have been futile and Christians would have been pitied more than all others. Resurrection assures Christians that their faith is secured in the living Christ. Through the resurrection, Christ conquered death. He is the "resurrection and life". In John 11:25-26, Jesus said, "I am the resurrection and the life. He who believes in me will live, even though he dies, and whoever lives and believes in me will never die". The reality and finality of death brought about by the first man, Adam's, disobedience have been overcome through the resurrection of Christ. 1 Corinthians 15:21-22 says, "For since death came through a man, the resurrection of the dead comes also through a man. For as in Adam, all die so in Christ all will be made alive".

Christ's resurrection provides Christians the evidence that God has ended the reign of death, and when the end comes, all those who belong to Christ will be raised in the same manner like Christ and death will be no more. 1 Corinthians 15:42-44 sums it up like this, "So will it be with the resurrection of the dead. The body that is sown is perishable, it is raised imperishable; it is sown in dishonour, it is raised in glory; it is sown in weakness, it is raised in power; it is sown a natural body, it is raised a spiritual body". The great commission is all about the resurrection of Jesus (Matt. 28:18-20). When you believe in Jesus Christ and put your faith in him, you chose life. Death through Adam, life through Jesus, ALLELUJAH.

The Gateways to the Heart Affect Our Faith. Watch out!

There are three gateways to the heart which include the mouth, the eyes, and the ears. The heart is the store room of faith. Each of these gateways can activate our faith or reduce our faith in the LORD. These gateways can also spark up fear which activates the devil just as faith activates God. We must be careful about what we hear, what we see, pass them through quality control, evaluate how they affect our believe and faith. We must evaluate what we hear and make sure that they are in line with what we believe. The story of the Promised Land is a good example of how the gateways can affect our faith. The news of the giants of Jericho sparked fear among the Israelites and the devil was activated. They forgot all what God did for them in Egypt. The miraculous signs and wonders of God in Egypt were all forgotten. The activation of the devil led to their disobedience and rebellion against God

(Num.14:1-4) despite the promises and assurances God had made to them which is summarised in Deuteronomy 1:29-30; "Do not be terrified; do not be afraid of them. The LORD your God, who is going before you, will fight for you, as he did for you in Egypt, before your eyes and in the desert. There you saw how the LORD your God carried you, as a father carries his son, all the way you went until you reached this place". The original intension when they left Egypt was for the Israelites to go to Mount Sinai to receive the law and then move on to Canaan. But because of their rebellion and disobedience, God's wrath was brought on them. Wandering in the wilderness for 40 years was part of the punishment. All those who were 20 years or more, who witnessed the miraculous signs of God in Egypt apart from Joshua and Caleb died in the wilderness (Num. 14:26-35). They never entered the Promised Land apart from their children.

Quite often, fear about our finances, not getting healing, our marriage, our children, and our security results in activating the devil which reduces our faith in God. We end up ignoring God's promises to us. Such fears activate the devil which sparks up evil desires in our hearts such as not waiting patiently for God's time with prayers, rebellion against God, corruption, stealing, cheating and other unrighteous acts, which make us become enemies of God. Christ constantly encourages us to cast our cares upon him (1 Peter 5:7), and to take His yoke upon us in exchange for our burdens (Matt. 11:28-30). Isaiah 28:16 says, "The one who trusts will never be dismayed". The Psalmist in Psalm 46:1-3 says, "God is our refuge and strength and ever present help in trouble. Therefore we will not fear, though the earth gives way and the mountains fall into the heart of the sea, though its waters roar and foam and the mountains quake with surging". Psalm 40:1-2 says, "I waited patiently for the LORD; he turned to me and heard my cry. He lifted me out of the slimy pit, out of the mud and mire; he set my feet on a rock and gave me a firm place to stand". Psalm 27:13 is telling us "Wait for the LORD; be strong and take heart and wait for the LORD". Faith on fire produces total victory.

The Word of Spirit and of Power

2 Corinthians 5:7

We live by faith, not by sight.

James 2:14, 17

What good is it my brothers, if a man claims to have faith but has no deeds? Can such faith save him? Faith by itself, if not accompanied by action is dead.

James 2:21-22, 24

Was not our ancestor Abraham considered righteous for what he did when he offered his son Isaac on the altar? You see that his faith and his actions were working together, and his faith was made complete by what he did. You see that a person is justified by what he does and not by faith alone.

Mathew 7:20-21

Thus by their fruit you will recognise them. Not everyone who says to me, Lord, Lord will enter the kingdom of heaven, but only he who does the will of my father who is in heaven.

Mathew 17:20

He replied "Because you have so little faith, I tell you the truth, if you have faith as small as mustard seed, you can say to this mountain, move from here to there and it will move. Nothing will be impossible for you".

1 Thessalonians 1:3

We continually remember before our God and Father your work produced by faith, your labour prompted by love and your endurance inspired by hope in our Lord Jesus Christ.

James 2:14, 17

What good is it, my brothers, if a man claims to have faith but no deeds? Can such faith save him? In the same way, faith by itself, if it is not accompanied by action, is dead.

2 Thessalonians 1:3, 11

We ought always to thank God for you, brothers, and rightly so, because your faith is growing more and the love every one of you has for each other is increasing. With this in mind, we constantly pray for you, that our God may count you worthy of his calling and that by his power, he may fulfill every good purpose of yours and every act prompted by your faith.

Chapter 17

ATTRIBUTES OF GOD

God is the creator of the universe and the redeemer of humanity. Meaningful profound knowledge of God makes believers love him and serve him better. It is through the understanding of the attributes of God that gives us the knowledge of who God is, his character and nature. From such knowledge, believers come to know the loving, glorious, gracious, compassionate and Holy God who is the only one worthy and rightly deserves our allegiance. In Jeremiah 9:23-24, the LORD says, "Let not the wise man boast of his wisdom or the strong man boast of his strength or the rich man boast of his riches, but let him who boasts boast about this; that he understands and knows me, that I am the LORD, who exercises kindness, justice and righteousness on earth, for in these I delight", declares the LORD. God is **Holy, Loving, Just, Righteous, Jealous, Merciful, Good, Patient** and **Faithful.**

Other Representative Descriptions of God's Character and Nature

The Bible uses many representative things to describe God's being and character. Some examples are: God is compared to a father who shows compassion and love to his children (Ps. 103:13). God is compared to a shepherd who cares for his sheep to demonstrate his nature of caring, provision of our needs and protection (Ps. 23:1-4). God is also compared to a potter for the work of his creation (Jer. 18:6). God is also likened to various images and things in nature to describe his character and nature. Some examples include: **Rock** (Ps. 18:2), **Light** (Ps. 27:1), **Fire** (Deut. 4:24), **Lion** (Hos. 11:10), **Eagle** (Deut. 32:11), **Anchor:** is likened to the security in the hope believers have in the certainty of God's promise (Heb. 6:19). The following images are also used in the Bible to demonstrate God's perfect protection: **Fortress, Shield, Horn, Stronghold** (Ps. 18:2).

Exodus 34:6-7 summarises God's attributes as follows: "The LORD, the LORD, the compassionate and gracious God, slow to anger, abounding in love and faithfulness, maintaining love to thousands and forgiving wickedness, rebellion and sin. Yet he does not leave the guilty unpunished; he punishes the children and their children for the sin of the fathers to the third and fourth generation". Better knowledge of the following attributes of God will increase awareness and loyalty to him and put him in first place in our lives.

Holy

God is the only one that is holy (1 Sam. 2:2). All that is associated with God is holy. God the Father is holy (John 17:11), God the son is holy (Acts 3:14), God's spirit is holy and bears the name 'Holy Spirit' (Ps. 51:11). God's name is holy (Luke 1:49), his words are holy (Ps. 105:42), his ways are holy (Ps. 77:13), his arm is holy (Ps. 98:1), his throne is holy (Ps. 47:8) and the angels surrounding the throne are 'Holy Ones' (Ps. 89:5). Because of His holiness, He must be acknowledged as Holy God (Lev. 22:32) and must be honoured (Lev. 10:3), worshipped (Ps. 96:9) and feared (Isa. 8:13). Holiness means separate from sin. God expects believers to be holy. Leviticus 11:45 says, "I am the LORD who brought you out of Egypt to be your God, therefore be holy, because I am holy". Because of God's character of holiness, he cannot tolerate sin in the lives of people, and he brings judgment to those who do not repent (Hab. 1:12-13). God makes us holy when we trust in Jesus (Heb. 10:10).

Loving

God is love (1 John 4:16). God demonstrated his love for us by giving his only son Jesus Christ as the sacrificial lamb to die for the sins of the world (John 3:16). 1 John 4:19 says, "We love because he first loved us". God expects us to follow the example of the sacrificial love of Christ (John 3:16). Jesus is our model of love. He came to serve and not to be served (Mark 10:42-45). God's love should motivate believers to repay evil with good (Rom. 12:14) and practice long-suffering and forgiveness towards those who do wrong to us (Matt. 18:21-35). 1 Corinthians 13:4-8 says, "Love is patient, love is kind, it does not envy, it does not boast, it is not proud. It is not rude, it is not self-seeking, it is not easily angered, and it keeps no record of wrongs. Love does not delight in evil but rejoices with the truth. It always protects, always trusts, always hopes, and always perseveres". Christ's love should motivate us to always act in the interest of others, and such act could bring them to God. Anyone who does not love has no true knowledge of God in him. (1 John 4:8). Whoever lives in love, lives in God, and God in him (1 John 4:16). If anyone says I love God, yet hates his brother, he is a liar. For anyone who does not love his brother, whom he has seen cannot love God, whom he has not seen (1 John 4:20).

Just

God is upright and just. All his ways are just (Deut. 32:4). The foundation of God's throne is built on righteousness and justice (Ps. 97:2). God loves justice and acts with justice (Ps. 33:5). He upholds justice for the oppressed (Ps. 103:6) in delivering justice. God is not partial (Job 34:18-19). God demonstrates his justice by judging us according to our deeds. The wicked will be punished and the righteous will be rewarded (Ezek. 18:20). As God wants believers to be Holy, he also wants them to practice justice in order to reflect his justice. Proverbs 21:3 says, "To do what is right and just is more acceptable to the LORD than sacrifice". God's love never conflicts with his justice. Love and justice were displayed in one event. Because of God's love for us, he gave his only son for us as a sacrificial lamb, and because of his justice, Christ died for our sins on the cross to make us stand justified before God (1 Tim. 2:5-6).

Righteous

God is righteous (John 17:25). He always does the right things and he does no wrong. The foundation of God's throne is built on righteousness and justice (Ps. 89:14). Psalm 119:137-138 says, "Righteous are you, O LORD and your laws are right". The statues you have laid down are righteous, they are fully trustworthy. God's acts are righteous (Judges 5:11), his judgments are righteous (Ps. 7:11) because he judges with righteousness (Ps. 96:13). His law and commandment are holy (Rom. 7:12). God is a righteous judge (2 Tim 4:8). His justice is not compromised in justifying sinners (Rom. 3:24-26), making his redemption action righteous. God rules over creation in righteousness and expects humans to conduct themselves in righteousness in their living (Rom. 14:17). Jesus Christ is the only sinless person who has ever lived on earth in conformity with the nature and will of God (Heb. 7:26). Because of his righteousness, he became the perfect sacrificial lamb who could die to save us. Through faith in Jesus, we are made righteous (Rom. 3:22-24).

Jealous

God is jealous and wants believers to worship him exclusively. Exodus 34:14 says, "Do not worship any other God, for the LORD whose name is Jealous is a jealous God". God is provoked when we worship idols and he responds with anger as can be seen in Nahum 1:2 which says, "The LORD is a jealous and avenging God; the LORD takes vengeance and is filled with wrath". Deuteronomy 32:16 says, "They made him jealous with foreign gods and angered him with their detestable idols". God does not want anything or any human being to share his glory. God is the only one that deserves our praise and loyalty. He wants first place in our lives. God's demand for our loyalty and first position in our lives extends to other things in our lives which get in our way in walking with God and giving him first place. Such things that could occupy first places in our lives could be: family, recreation, holiday, career, friends, birthdays, hobbies, loyalty to country, church activities, just to mention but a few. Things as family, career, and church activities are good but they are among the things that get in our way in giving God the first place he deserves in our lives. When we give our allegiance to idols, we place God in a secondary position in our lives. God does not want any competition for our love and loyalty. The fundamental sin then is for people to be 'double minded' in trusting God and giving him first place in their lives. The temptation to try to be friends with God and friends with the world at the same time is nothing less than spiritual adultery. Anyone who chooses to be a friend of the world becomes an enemy of God (James 4:4). For believers to give God the first place in their lives, having a priority list for the Christian journey should be a wise thing to have, starting with the following examples:

Priority List for a Christian	Priority List for a Pastor
1. I am a Christian and I have a relationship with my God.	1. I am a Christian and I have a relationship with my God.
2. I am a husband and I have a relationship with my wife.	2. I am a husband and I have a relationship with my wife.
3. I am a father and I have a relationship with my children.	3. I am a father and I have a relationship with my children.
4. I am a worker and I have a relationship with my employer.	4. I am a worker and I have a relationship with my employer.
5. I am a church goer and I have a relationship with my church.	5. I am a pastor and I have a relationship with my church.
6. I am a member of a family and I have a relationship with my family.	6. I am a member of a family and I have a relationship with my family.
7. I am a member of a community and I have a relationship with my community.	7. I am a member of a community and I have a relationship with my community
8. I am a citizen and I have a relationship with my country.	8. I am a citizen and I have a relationship with my country.
9. Others	9. Others

The choice depends on individual Christian priorities. But God is number 1 on the list and it must remain permanent in the life of a Christian.

Merciful

God is merciful. He does not punish us as our sins deserve because of his mercy. While the 'wages of sin is death' but because of his mercy, God sent his only son, Jesus Christ to the cross to save sinners (Rom. 5:8). God's mercy made it possible for believers to receive "the gift of God which is eternal life in Christ Jesus our Lord" (Rom. 6:23). God's mercy has been shown in his faithfulness to the covenants he made with Israel. Deuteronomy 4:31 says, "For the LORD your God is a merciful God; he will not abandon or destroy you or forsake the covenant with your forefathers which he confirmed to them by oath". The afflicted, those in need, the oppressed, the weak call on God for mercy, and he never fails to show mercy to them (Ps. 123:2-4). Hebrews 4:16 says, "Let us approach the throne of grace with confidence, so that we may receive mercy and find grace to help us in our time of need". Psalm 68:5 says, "God is a Father to the fatherless, a defender of widows". Sinners call on God's mercy for forgiveness. Psalm 51:1 says, "Have mercy on me, O God, according to your unfailing love, according to your great compassion blot out my transgressions". It is through God's mercy that we are declared righteous through Jesus Christ (Titus 3:5).

Jesus Christ is a model of God's merciful attribute. Jesus' miracles were driven by his merciful nature (Matt. 9:36). His merciful nature was demonstrated on the cross when he prayed for forgiveness for those who crucified him (Luke 23:34). As in other attributes believers share with God, they are expected to live the same life of mercy towards other people. The number eight blessing in the beatitudes is mercy which says in Matthew 5:7, "Blessed are the merciful, for they will be shown mercy". In Luke 6:36 Jesus says, "Be merciful just as your Father is merciful". The parable of the Good Samaritan (Luke 10:25-37) is a good example of how to show mercy to the afflicted. The pagan Samaritan showed mercy to the afflicted thereby demonstrating a true neighbourly love. The Levi and the priest never cared. They did not see beyond the religious activity in the tabernacle and the church. In Matthew 9:13, Jesus' answer to the Pharisees points to the fact that the merciful life of believers should come before their religious life. "God have mercy on me" is a common expression of believers when they go through trials. As a father has compassion on his children, so the LORD has compassion on those who fear him (Ps. 103:13).

Good

God is good. In Luke 18:19, Jesus tells us that "No one is good except God alone". We experience his goodness in his love, mercy, patience, grace, provision, kindness, compassion, faithfulness, righteousness and perfection. Every good thing we experience and enjoy in creation is from the goodness of God. 1 Timothy 4:4 says, "For everything God created is good, and nothing is to be rejected if it is received with thanksgiving, because it is consecrated by the word of God and prayer". God's goodness is reflected in his actions (Ps. 119:68), in his promises to believers (Josh. 23:14-15), in his love (Ps. 86:5) and in his creation (1 Tim 4:4). In all things, God works for the good of those who love him, who have been called according to his purpose (Rom. 8:28). The LORD is good to all, he has compassion on all he has made (Ps. 145:9). Good and upright is the LORD (Ps. 25:8). God saw all that he has made and it was very good (Gen. 1:31). Jesus is the good shepherd. He lays down his life for his sheep (John 10:11).

Patience

God is patient. He is "slow to anger" (Num. 14:18). The phrase "slow to anger" is a common expression in describing God's patience as can be seen in Psalm 86:15, Nehemiah 9:17, Joel 2:13, Exodus 34:6, Psalm 103:8. God's patience allows people to come to repentance and come back to him. 2 Peter 3:9 says, "The Lord is not slow in keeping his promise, as some understand slowness. He is patient with you, not wanting anyone to perish, but everyone to come to repentance". In the case of the sinful people of Nineveh, God's patience led then to repentance. In Jonah 3:9-10, the King of Nineveh said, "Who knows? God may yet relent and with compassion turn from his fierce anger so that we will not perish". When God saw what they did and how they turned from their evil ways, he had compassion and did not bring upon them the destruction he had threatened.

The forty years of disobedience of the Israelites in the desert (Acts 13:18) show that God is patient for a long time with sinful people. He endured their misconduct for forty years.

Believers are urged to show patience to others (Eph. 4:2) just as God is patient with us. Christian leadership should be a model of faith, patience, love, endurance, persecutions and sufferings (2 Tim. 3:10).

Faithful

God is faithful and this has been demonstrated in all his promises by fulfilling them. In Deuteronomy 7:9 it says, "Know therefore that the LORD your God is God; he is the faithful God, keeping his covenant of love to a thousand generations of those who love him and keep his commands". Joshua 23:14 says, "Now I am about to go the way of all the Earth. You know with all your heart and soul that not one of all the good promises the LORD your God gave you has failed. Every promise has been fulfilled, no one has failed". All the promises God made to Abraham were fulfilled (Gen. 12:2-3). Hebrews 6:13-15 says, When God made his promise to Abraham, since there was no one greater for him to swear by, he swore by himself saying, "I will surely bless you and give you many descendants". And so after waiting patiently, Abraham received what was promised. God's promise to Solomon, son of King David to build the temple for his name was fulfilled (1 Kings 8:17-21). God's promises are yes and settled. The promise in the Old Testament of the coming of the Messiah (Jesus Christ) was fulfilled (Acts 13:32-33). God does not change. What he says in the Bible is the truth. If we put our trust in him, he is faithful to his words. When we face trials, we can trust and rely completely on his faithfulness.

Chapter 18

JESUS' MISSION

1. He Came to Reveal the Father

Jesus is a model of attributes of God. We start knowing God when we know Jesus Christ. We know God in the person and work of Jesus Christ. Our relationship with God starts and ends with Jesus. Christ is the bridge that connects us to the Father.

What Does the Bible Say?

John 1:18

No one has ever seen God, but God the only son who is at the Father's side has made him known.

John 12:44-45

Then Jesus cried out, "When a man believes in me, he does not believe in me only, but in the one who sent me. When he looks at me, he sees the one who sent me.

Colossians 1:15-17

He is the image of the invisible God, the firstborn over all creation. For by him all things were created; things in heaven and on earth, visible and invisible whether thrones or powers or rulers or authorities; all things were created by him and for him. He is before all things, and in him all things hold together.

Hebrews 1:3

The son is the radiance of God's glory and the exact representation of his being sustaining all things by his powerful Word. After he had provided purification for sins, he sat down at the right hand of the Majesty in heaven.

2. He Came to Redeem Fallen Mankind

Sin was responsible for the fall of the first man, Adam. He disobeyed God (Gen 3:5). Due to his disobedience all the original cordial relationships with God were broken. Mankind no longer enjoyed the blessings of intimate relationship with God. Mankind became enemy of God, and came under the curse of God's judgment, and became unworthy to stand before God. Because of human disobedience, the whole creation was thrown into darkness. Despite the covenants God made with Israel's leaders, they were constantly broken. God's covenant with David is part of God's plan to save Israel from sin through Jesus (2 Sam. 7:12-16). Because of God's love for his people, he refused to give up on them. He promised to raise up a servant who would suffer for the sins of his people. He will atone for their sins (Isaiah 52:13, 53:12). God's plan to finally put away the sins of the world came when the conception and birth of Jesus were announced and revealed that he would "save his people from their sins" (Matt. 1:21).

The first man, Adam and Israel were disobedient sons of God, but Jesus became the obedient son of God. He gave his life as a ransom for many (Mark 10:45).

The resurrection of Jesus Christ is fundamental to the Christian "faith". It is a proof that he has cleared his believers from their sins (Rom. 4:25, 1 Cor. 15:17). All who are identified with Christ by faith are forgiven and justified before God (Rom. 3:21-26). What neither the law nor blood of bulls and goats could do, Jesus Christ did it with his own blood (Rom. 8:3-4).

The Good News

After his resurrection and ascension, Jesus Christ followers began to proclaim the "Good news" (the gospel) of what Jesus did, and calling people to repent and be baptized in the name of Jesus

111

Christ for forgiveness of their sins (Acts 2:38). Although believers continue to struggle with sin in this life (Gal. 5:16-23), sin is no longer a master of them (Rom. 6:1-23). The Holy Spirit empowers them to fight sin.

What Does the Bible Say?

Mathew 1:21

She will give birth to a son and you will give him the name "Jesus" because he will save his people from their "sins".

1 John 3:5

But you know that he appeared so that he might take away our sins. And in him is no sin.

1 Peter 2:24

He himself bore our sins in his body on the tree, so that we might die to sins and live for righteousness.

Acts 13:38-39

Therefore my brothers, I want you to know that through Jesus the forgiveness of sins is proclaimed to you. Through him everyone who believed is justified from everything you could not be justified from the Law of Moses.

1 John 2:12

I write to you dear children, because your sins have been forgiven on account of his name.

Romans 5:19

For just as through the disobedience of the one man, the many were made sinners, so also through the obedience of the one man the many will be made righteous.

Romans 8:3-4

For what the law was powerless to do in that it was weakened by the sinful nature, God did by sending his own son in the likeness of sinful man to be sin offering. And so he condemned sin in sinful man in order that the righteous requirements of the law might be fully met in us, who do not live according to the sinful nature but according to the Spirit.

3. He Came to Revive the Faltering Hope of Those Who Were Looking for the Messiah.

The expectation for a Messiah by Israel was due to the promise God made to David (2 Samuel 7:12-16). God promised David that from his offspring he would raise up a king that would reign forever on his throne. During the reign of David and his son Solomon, Israel prospered and became a great nation possessing the land promised to Abraham. The temple was built under king Solomon's reign. The Messiah was looked upon as a son of David who will destroy the enemies and oppressors of Israel. Hope for the promised Messiah was on Solomon but Solomon sinned against God's commandments given to the kings of Israel. Due to God's punishment, the kingdom was divided into two. Israel was no longer one nation (1 Kings 10-11).

The testimony that Jesus is the promised Messiah is affirmed in the scripture by Jesus himself and others. In Mark 12:35-37, Jesus redefines the long-established understanding of the messiah as the son of David. In Mark 8:30, Jesus affirms that he is the Messiah. He says he is the Messiah through whom redemption will come to many (Mark 10:45). He came not to defeat the enemies and oppressors of Israel but to bring victory over satan, sin and death. In Acts 5:42 and 9:22, Peter and Saul (Paul) affirm that Jesus is the promised Messiah. Jesus is now ascended and exalted king in heaven sitting at the right hand of God in fulfillment of his early ministry prediction in Mark 14:62.

What Does the Bible Say?

Mark 12:35-37

While Jesus was teaching in the temple courts, he asked, "Why do teachers of the law say that the Messiah is the son of David?

113

David himself speaking by the Holy Spirit declared: "The Lord said to my Lord: sit at my right hand until I put your enemies under your feet". David himself calls him "Lord". How then can he be his son?

Mark 8:31

He then began to teach them that the son of Man must suffer many things and be rejected by the elders, the chief priests and the teachers of the law, and that he must be killed and after three days rise again.

Mark 14:62

"I am", said Jesus "And you will see the son of Man sitting at the right hand of the Mighty one and coming on the clouds of heaven".

Mark 8:29

"But what about you? He asked. Who do you say I am?" Peter answered, "You are the Messiah".

Acts 5:42

Day after day in the temple courts and from house to house and they never stopped teaching and proclaiming the good news that Jesus is the Messiah.

Acts 9:22

Yet Saul grew more and more powerful and baffled the Jews living in Damascus by proving that Jesus is the Messiah.

Acts 2:34-36

For David did not ascent to heaven, and yet he said, "The Lord said to my Lord, sit at my right hand until I make your enemies a footstool for your feet". Therefore let all Israel be assured of this: God has made this Jesus, whom you crucified, both Lord and Messiah.

John 4:25-26

The woman said; "I know that Messiah called Jesus is coming. When he comes, he will explain everything to us". Then Jesus declared, "I, who speak to you I am he".

Mathew 26:63-64

But Jesus remained silent. The high priest said to him, "I charge you under oath by the living God: Tell us if you are the Messiah, the son of God". "You have said so". Jesus replied. "But I say to all of you; from now on you will see the son of Man sitting at the right hand of the Mighty One and coming on the clouds of heaven".

Mark 14:61-62

Again the high priest asked him, "are you the Messiah, the son of the Blessed one?' "I am" said Jesus. And you will see the son of Man sitting at the right hand of the Mighty one and coming on the clouds of heaven".

Isaiah 9:6-7

For to us a child is born, to us a son is given and the government will be on his shoulders. And he will be called Wonderful Counselor, Mighty God; Everlasting Father, Prince of Peace. Of the increase of his government and peace there will be no end. He will reign on David's throne and over his Kingdom, establishing and upholding it with justice and righteousness from that time on and for ever.

4. He Introduced Us to the Power of the Holy Spirit

Jesus did not leave us alone. He sent the helper to us. The Pentecost is a testimony of the Holy Spirit that he sent to us, to comfort us and guide us in the spirit controlled way of living. The Holy Spirit is God's presence in our midst.

What Does the Bible Say?

John 14:16-17

I will ask the Father and he will give you another counselor to be with you forever – the spirit of truth. The world cannot accept

him, because it neither sees him nor knows him. But you know
him, for he lives with you and will be in you.

Acts 2:1-4

When the day of Pentecost came, they were altogether in one
place. Suddenly, a sound like the blowing of a violent wind came
from heaven and filled the whole house where they were sitting.
They saw what seemed to be tongues of fire that separated and
came to rest on each of them. All of them were filled with the Holy
Spirit and began to speak in other tongues as the Spirit enabled
them.

5. He Came To Teach Us How to Love and Forgive Each Other

Christ is the model of sacrificial love because he saved us by
paying for our sins by his death on the cross (Mark 10:42-45). His
love provides an example to us and should motivate us to practice
sacrificial love towards others (Matt. 22:39; John 3:16). Jesus'
love teaches us to repay evil with good (Rom. 12:14).

Jesus' love teaches us to be patient, practice long-suffering with
others and forgive those who wrong us (Matt. 18:21-35). Jesus'
love teaches us to always act in the best interests of others (1 Cor.
13:4-8), hoping that they may repent and believe in Jesus Christ and
become reconciled with God (Matt. 4:17; 2 Tim. 2:24-26).

6. He Came To Teach Us How to Pray

Jesus' prayer life is a model for believers. He encourages us to
pray persistently, continuously and not give up (Luke 18:1-8).

Jesus and his disciples provided us with examples of how to
pray (Luke 23:34, Acts 7:60). Jesus wants us to pray for our
enemies (Matt. 5:44).

Jesus prayed before taking important decisions (Luke 6:12-
13). At crises times, Jesus prayed (Matt. 26:36-44; Luke 3:21;
9:29; John 12:27).

Jesus' prayer life taught us that he offered prayer that was not answered (Luke 22:41-44) and prayers that were answered (Heb. 5:7). Also Jesus wrestled in prayer (Luke 22:41-44, Heb. 5:7), showing us example to pray relentlessly. Jesus prayed for his disciples and believers (John 17:6-26; Luke 22:32).

Jesus ascended into heaven and continues to intercede for us (Heb. 7:25).

Jesus' priesthood is forever and because he has experienced trials and sufferings, he is able to sympathize with us in our troubles. In heaven he becomes the perfect mediator between us and God, making his intercession for us more valid (Heb. 7:25).

Jesus sent the Holy Spirit to us as our counsellor to guide and equip us. The Holy Spirit plays an important part in our prayer life (Rom 8:15). Also the Holy Spirit Himself intercedes for us (Rom. 8:26) and it is by Him we cry out "Abba Father" (Rom. 8:15). Believers are advised to pray in the Spirit always (Eph. 6:18; 1 Cor. 14:15; Jude 20). Prayer to God is to be made "In The Name Of Jesus" (John 14:13; 15:16; Matt. 18:19-20). Jesus told the disciples to address God as "Father" (Rom. 8:15; Gal 4:6). Furthermore, God is not just "Father" but "Father in heaven" (Matt. 6:9).

7. He Came To Give Us Assurance of Life after Death

Mankind has been held hostage all their lives due to fear of death. Jesus came to set us free from fear of death through his death and resurrection. All who believe in him will live even though they die (John 11:25-26). The resurrection of Christ is the foundation of the Christian faith. As Apostle Paul puts it, "If Christ did not rise, then the Christian faith is futile and Christians are to be pitied more than other people" (1Cor. 15:17-19). Adam's disobedience brought sin and death to the world. Christ death and resurrection conquered death and sin (1 Cor. 15:21-22).

The resurrection of Christ provided evidence that God has put an end to the reign of death. The resurrection affirmed the hope for the coming of the end when all who belong to Christ will be raised from death in the same manner like Christ (John 11:24-25) and there will be no more death. In 2 Timothy 1:10 Apostle Paul says, "But it has now been revealed through the appearing of our saviour Christ Jesus who has destroyed death and has brought life and immortality to light through the gospel". Eternal life has been made available to all who believe in Jesus (John 11:24-25). In Romans 8:11, Apostle Paul also says, "And if the Spirit of him who raised Jesus from the dead is living in you, he who raised Christ from the dead will also give life to your mortal bodies through his Spirit who lives in you".

What Does the Bible Say?

John 11:25-26

Jesus said to her, "I am the resurrection and the life. He who believes in me will live, even though he dies; and whoever lives and believes in me will never die. Do you believe this?"

1 Corinthians 15:21-22

For since death came through a man, the resurrection of the dead comes also through a man. For as in Adam all die, so in Christ all will be made alive.

John 11:24-25

Martha answered, "I know he will rise again in the resurrection at the last day". Jesus said to her, "I am the resurrection and the life. He who believes in me will live even though he dies".

2 Timothy 1:10

But it has now been revealed through the appearing of our savior, Christ Jesus, who has destroyed death and has brought life and immortality to light through the gospel.

8. He Came To Assure Us of Heaven.

The ultimate hope for believers is to be in heaven with Christ. In Mathew 5:12, he promises that believers' reward will be in heaven.

Believers are required to live their earthly live with the end in mind by storing up treasures in heaven (Phil. 3:20). believers' hope at death is to depart and be with Christ, which is better by far (Phil. 1:23). In the present age, our citizenship is in heaven (Phil. 3:20). Christ is currently in heaven and believers who are already asleep (dead) are already with Christ in heaven awaiting his return, when God will bring with Jesus those who have fallen asleep in him (Phil.1:21-24; 1 Thess.4:14). Believers are looking forward to a new heaven and a new earth, the home of righteousness (2 Peter 3:13).

What Does the Bible Say?

Mathew 5:12

Rejoice and be glad, because great is your reward in heaven, for in the same way they persecuted the prophets who were before you.

Mathew 6:20

But store up for yourselves treasures in heaven, where moth and rust do not destroy, and where thieves do not break in and steal.

Philippians 3:20

But our citizenship is in heaven. And we eagerly await a saviour from there, the Lord Jesus Christ.

Philippians 1:23

I am torn between the two: I desire to depart and be with Christ, which is better by far.

1 Thessalonians 4:14

We believe that Jesus died and rose again and so we believe that God will bring with Jesus those who have fallen asleep in him.

9. He Came To Get Us Ready For The Last Day On Earth.

Our journey on earth will end at some point in time when our mission on earth is fulfilled. Death is inevitable. We will depart this earth and be with Christ which is gain. Death is a journey not a destination. It is the process which we go through to the other side. Death for believers is a shadow not a reality. Death is lonely but you are never alone. In our living we should not lose sight of the end. We should not live as if this life has no end. Jesus advises us to watch out and always be prepared to meet him when he returns. 1 Thessalonians 4:13-14 says, "Brothers, we do not want you to be ignorant about those who fall asleep, or to grieve like the rest of men, who have no hope. We believe that Jesus died and rose again and so we believe that God will bring with Jesus those who have fallen asleep in him. Nobody knows when but he expects believers to be ready to receive him when he comes back. He wants believers to be faithful and practice wise living which is living with the end in mind (Matt. 24:45-51). When He finally comes, believers should not worry or be afraid. Christ said that in his father's house there are many rooms to accommodate them and he has gone there to prepare to receive them (John 14:1-3).

What Does the Bible Say?

John 14:1-3

"Do not let your hearts be troubled. Trust in God, trust also in me. In my father's house are many rooms; if it were not so, I would have told you. I am going there to prepare a place for you. I will come back and take you to be with me that you also may be where I am".

Mathew 24:42-44

"Therefore keep watch, because you do not know on what day your Lord will come. But understand this: if the owner of the house had known at what time of night the thief was coming, he would have kept watch and would not have let his house be broken into. So you also must be ready, because the son of Man will come at an hour you do not expect him".

Chapter 19

THE REDEMPTION THAT CAME THROUGH JESUS CHRIST COVERS PAST AND PRESENT SINS

All Have Sinned and Fallen Short

Even those prominent names in the Bible who were after the heart of God at some point sinned. Isaiah 53:6 says, "We all, like sheep, have gone astray, each of us has turned to his own way, and the LORD has laid on him the iniquity of us all". For example, Noah, a man of the soil, proceeded to plant a vineyard. When he drank some of its wine, he became drunk (Gen. 9:20-21), Abram said to his wife Sarai, "Say that you are my sister, so that I will be treated well for your sake" (Gen. 12:13). Then Isaac said to Jacob, "Are you really my son, Esau?" "I am," he replied (Genesis 27:24). The men of Israel sampled their provisions but did not inquire of the LORD. Then Joshua made a treaty of peace with them (Josh. 9:14-15). For they rebelled against the Spirit of God and rash words came from Moses's lips (Ps. 106:33). David had done what was right in the eyes of the LORD and had not failed to keep any of the LORD's commands all the days of his life except in the case of Uriah the Hittite (1 Kings 15:5). These prominent names in the Bible were all commended for their faith (Heb. 11:39), and are justified freely by his grace through the redemption that came through Christ Jesus (Rom. 3:24).

God sent his son as an atoning sacrifice for our sins (1 John 4:10). He did not spare his son, but gave him up for us all (Rom. 8:32). The atoning sacrifice of the son was very necessary because the finality is that Old Testament sacrificial system could not have ultimately provided true atonement because

Hebrews 10:4 says, "Because it is impossible for the blood of bulls and goats to take away sins". 1 Peter 3:18 says, "For Christ died for sins once for all, the righteous for the unrighteousness, to bring you to God".

Christ's earthly life shows that he is the only sinless person who has ever lived (2 Cor. 5:21) and this with his active obedience (John 10:15,18) qualified him to be the perfect sacrifice. His death provided atonement for our sins. God raised him to life for our justification (Rom. 4:25).

Atonement in the Old Testament

The sacrificial system in the Old Testament was the means through which sins were atoned for. The process is as follows:

Two male goats are used in the atonement for sin. Lots are cast to pick both the goats for sin offering for the Lord and the goat to be used as the scapegoat. The goat for the sin offering is slaughtered and the blood is used for the atonement for the sins of the offerer. This process restores ritual purity which leads to forgiveness of the sins of the offerer and thus re-establishes cordial relationship between God and the offerer (Lev. 16:6-19). The scapegoat is presented to God alive. The offerer and his family make confessions of their sins, passing them on to the scapegoat. A very fit person then leads the scapegoat very far into the desert making sure that it has no chance of returning back to the offerer. It is assumed that if the scapegoat finds its way back, the sins will be passed back to the offerer.

Atonement in the New Testament

Atonement in the New Testament is the reconciliation of God and mankind through the death of Jesus Christ. God's disposition about sin is not different from that of the Old Testament. He still considers those who are sinful and unrighteous his enemies (Rom. 5:10, Col. 1:21). In the New Testament, Jesus Christ is the sacrificial lamb. He died for us on the cross as our sin offering. He did not have any sin to die for. Christ's earthly life and perfect obedience qualifies him as the perfect sacrificial lamb. Because of God's love for us, he did not spare his son but gave him up for us all (Rom. 8:32).

In John 10:15 and Hebrews 9:14, Jesus was a willing lamb and was involved in the accomplishment of the atonement by his death. His resurrection is a testimony of God's acceptance of Christ's sacrifice.

The Old Testament sacrifices could not have adequately provided the necessary atonements for sin. Hebrews 10:4 says, "It is impossible for the blood of bulls and goats to take away sins". Hence, the atoning sacrifice of Jesus Christ on the cross was necessary because God loves us and the world (1 John 2:2).

Jesus' atoning sacrifice by his death on the cross ended the Old Testament sacrificial system which involves animal and grain offerings.

Falling Back into Sin

Believers are baptized into Christ and have clothed themselves with Christ (Gal. 3:27). We must go on to maturity and not continue in sin. The new nature has overtaken the old and not laying again the foundation of redemption from acts that lead to death. The wages of sin is death, but the gift of God is eternal life in Christ Jesus our Lord. You cannot continue in sin because it was not with perishable things, such as silver or gold that you were redeemed from the empty way of life handed down to you from your forefathers but with the precious blood of Christ, a lamb without blemish or defect (1 Peter 1:18-19). It is impossible for those who have once been enlightened, who have tasted the heavenly gift, who have shared in the Holy Spirit, who have tasted the goodness of the word of God and powers of the coming age, if they fall away, to be brought back to repentance, because to their loss, they are crucifying the son of God all over again and subjecting him to public disgrace (Heb. 6:4-6).

The Word of Spirit and of Power

Leviticus 17:11

For the life of a creature is in the blood, and I have given it to you to make atonement for yourselves on the altar; it is the blood that makes atonement for one's life.

Hebrews 9:22

In fact, the law requires that nearly everything be cleansed with blood and without the shedding of blood there is no forgiveness.

Romans 5:8-9

But God demonstrates his own love for us in this: while we were still sinners, Christ died for us. Since we have now been justified by his blood, how much more shall we be saved from God's wrath through him.

1 John 3:9

No one who is born of God will continue to sin, because God's seed remains in him; he cannot go on sinning, because he has been born of God.

Mathew 20:28

Just as the son of Man did not come to be served, but to serve and to give his life as a ransom for many.

Hebrews 9:13-14

The blood of goats and bulls and the ashes of a heifer sprinkled on those who are ceremonially unclean sanctify them so that they are outwardly clean. How much more, then will the blood of Christ who through the eternal spirit offered himself unblemished to God, cleanse our consciences from acts that lead to death, so that we may serve the living God.

Isaiah 53:7

He was oppressed and afflicted, yet he did not open his mouth; He was led like a lamb to the slaughter and as sheep before her shearers is silent, so he did not open his mouth.

John 10:15,18

Just as the Father knows me and I know the Father – and I lay down my life for the sheep. No one takes it from me, but I lay it down of my own accord. I have the authority to lay it down and authority to take it up again.

Chapter 20

BIBLE PASSAGES AND COMMENTS THAT EXPLAIN THE LORD'S PRAYER

Jesus is our prayer model. He showed us how to pray (Matt. 6:9-13; Luke 11:1-4). In Matthew 6:9 He says, "This then is how you should pray":

1. Our Father in Heaven
2. Hallowed be your Name
3. Your kingdom come
4. Your will be done on Earth as is in Heaven
5. Give us today our daily bread
6. Forgive us our sins, as we forgive those who sin against us
7. Lead us not into temptation but deliver us from evil
8. For the kingdom, the power and the glory are yours now and forever
9. Amen

Brief Comments

Out of the seven prayer points in Matthew 6:9-13, the first three address God; the other 4 are related to human needs and concerns. As the Christian journey will always involve trials and hurdles, the Lord's Prayer has become a handy and inspirational tool for devotion among Christians for two millennia. It is easily committed to memory and seen as not just a prayer for the few privileged group, but for all who call on God as their Father through Jesus Christ, our Lord and Saviour. The prayer demonstrates the love of God for Christians and wants us to rely and trust God in the supply of our day to day needs. The prayer is simple, evoking and can easily be committed to memory. God in his wisdom may allow Christians to go through trials but for a purpose that is beneficial to us. God uses such trials to test our faith and strengthen our reliance and trust in him. Numbers 8 and 9 are concluding doxology which gives glory to God. It is not part of the New Testament text, but was included very early on. The doxology is often included at the end of the prayer by Protestants. Each prayer point is discussed as follows:

1. Our Father in Heaven (Matt 6:9)

Invocation of God as a Father is to give him the honour for He is the creator of the world and a loving father having authority over all creation. Faith in Jesus Christ gives believers the right to become sons of God and are also given the right to address God as 'Father' (Gal. 3:26). When praying, God is to be addressed not only as 'Father' but as 'Our Father in Heaven' (Matt. 6:9).

The following scriptures also confirm our sonship:

Romans 8:15-16

For you did not receive a spirit that makes you a slave again to fear, but you received the spirit of sonship. And by him, we cry "Abba Father". The Spirit himself testifies with our spirit that we are God's children.

Galatians 4:4-5

But when the time had fully come, God sent his son, born of a woman, born under law, to redeem those under law, that we might receive the full rights of sons.

Galatians 4:6-7

Because you are sons, God sent the Spirit of his son into our hearts, the Spirit who calls out "Abba Father". So you are no longer a slave, but a son, and since you are a son, God has made you also an heir.

Galatians 3:26

You are all sons of God through faith in Christ Jesus.

John 20:17

Jesus said, "Do not hold on to me, for I have not yet returned to the Father. Go instead to my brothers and tell them, I am retuning to my Father and your Father, to my God and your God".

2 Corinthians 6:17-18

Therefore come out from them and be separate, says the Lord. Touch no unclean thing, and I will receive you. I will be a father to you, and you will be my sons and daughters.

2. Hallowed Be Your Name (Matt 6:9)

An attribute of God is Holiness, righteousness, and a jealous God. Everything associated with Him is Holy. God the Father is Holy (John 17:11) as is the Son (Acts 3:14). God's Spirit is named "Holy Spirit". God's name is Holy (Luke 1:49). God's throne is Holy. Ascribe to the LORD the glory due to his name. Worship the LORD in the splendor of his Holiness. He must be honoured and feared.

What Does the Bible Say?

1 Samuel 2:2

There is no one holy like the Lord. There is no one besides you. There is no Rock like our God.

Exodus 34:14; 15:11

Do not worship any other god, for the LORD, whose name is Jealous, is a jealous God. Who among the gods is like you O LORD? Who is like you – majestic in holiness, awesome in glory, working wonders?

Revelation 4:8

Each of the four living creatures had six wings and was covered with eyes all around, even under his wings. Day and night they never stopped saying, "Holy, holy, holy is the Lord God Almighty, who was, and is, and is to come".

1 Chronicles 16:29

Ascribe to the LORD the glory due to his name. Worship the Lord in the splendor of his holiness.

Isaiah 6:1-3

I saw the Lord seated on a throne, high and exalted, and the train of his robe filled the temple. Above him were seraphs, each with six wings. With two wings they covered their faces, with two they covered their feet, and with two they were flying. And they were calling to one another: Holy, holy, holy is the LORD God Almighty, the whole earth is full of his glory.

3. Your Kingdom Come (Matt. 6:10)

The coming of the Kingdom of God is inevitable and it will come at God's own appointed time. The Kingdom of God is associated with the return of Jesus Christ. This prayer is a request for God to finally establish his Kingdom on earth. Jesus tells his believers that signs of the end of the age point to his return and will also show that the Kingdom of God is near (Luke 21:31). Jesus in John 3:5 answered, "I tell you the truth, no one can enter the Kingdom of God unless he is born of water and the Spirit". Christians are expected to be ready for the return of Jesus Christ and be prepared always, living in Christlikeness which reflects love, humility, obedience, justice and forgiveness (Matt. 5:14-16). When he comes Christians will account for how they used the material resources and opportunities given to them (Luke 19:11-27). Christians are encouraged to use their material resources to promote the work of the Kingdom of God.

What Does The Bible Say?

John 3:5

Jesus answered, "I tell you the truth, no one can enter the Kingdom of God unless, he is born of water and the Spirit."

1 Corinthians 15:24

Then the end will come, when he hands over the Kingdom to God the Father after he has destroyed all dominion, authority and power.

Mark 13:32-33, 37

No one knows about that day or hour, not even the angels in heaven nor the son, but only the Father. Be on guard. Be alert. You do not know when that time will come. What I say to you I say to everyone. Watch.

Luke 9:1-2

When Jesus had called the Twelve together, he gave them power and authority to drive out all demons and to cure diseases, and he sent them out to preach the Kingdom of God and to heal the sick.

Acts 14:22

Strengthening the disciples and encouraging them to remain true to the faith. "We must go through many hardships to enter the Kingdom of God" they said.

Luke 13:28-29

There will be weeping there, and gnashing of teeth, when you see Abraham, Isaac and Jacob and all the prophets in the Kingdom of God, but you yourselves thrown out.

Luke 14:15

When one of those at the table with him heard this, he said to Jesus, "Blessed is the man who will eat at the feast in the Kingdom of God".

Luke 21:31

Even so, when you see these things happening, you know that the kingdom of God is near.

Luke 22:15-18

And he said to them, "I have eagerly desired to eat this Passover with you before I suffer. For I tell you, I will not eat it again until it finds fulfillment in the Kingdom of God". After taking the cup, he gave thanks and said, "Take this and divide this among you. For I tell you I will not drink again from the fruit of the wine until the Kingdom of God comes".

Luke 10:9

Heal the sick who are there and tell them "The Kingdom of God is near you".

Mathew 24:14

And this gospel of the kingdom will be preached in the whole world as a testimony to all nations, and then the end will come.

4. Your Will be Done on Earth as is in Heaven (Matt. 6:10)

This prayer is a petition to our Father in heaven for his will in heaven to be done on earth. God's will is in the Bible. God's will is that you love your God with all your heart, all your soul, all your mind, and with all your strength. Secondly, love your neighbour as you love yourself (Mark 12:30-31). God in heaven does not want any soul to get lost. He wants everyone to be saved. When one is saved, God does not want him to live his earthly life for evil human desires, but rather for the will of God which is getting rid of all moral filth. It is God's will that you should be Holy (1 Thess. 4:3). The world and its desires will pass away but the man who does the will of God lives forever (1 John 2:17).

What the Bible Says:

Mathew 18:14

In the same way, your Father in heaven is not willing that any of these little ones should be lost.

1 Peter 1:16

For it is written, "Be Holy because I am Holy".

Mark 3:34-35

Then he looked at those seated in a circle around him and said, "Here are my mother and my brothers. Whoever does God's will is my brother and my sister and my mother."

5. Give Us Today Our Daily Bread (Matt. 6:11)

This prayer is for the provision of our daily physical needs. As a faithful and loving Father, he is sufficient for our daily needs. We are assured that he gives what is needed but not always what is wanted. In John 6:35, then Jesus declared, "I am the bread of life. He who comes to me will never go hungry and he who believes in me will never be thirsty". Bread is a powerful basic need for sustenance and life (John 6:26). God sustains us in our time of need as a demonstration of his fatherly love and compassion. God is involved in both the spiritual and physical needs of people. We humans are also expected to be concerned with the physical needs of fellow human beings. Trust God for the supply of your daily needs. Do not trust the world, because the world will disappoint you.

6. Forgive Us Our Sins as We Forgive Those Who Sin Against Us (Matt. 6:12)

This prayer is focused on mutual forgiveness among Christians based on which God also forgives. The prayer is not asking God to forgive people who in turn will forgive others, instead in reverse; the prayer is asking God to forgive us in the same way that we forgive one another or on the basis of our forgiving each other. In Colossians Paul writes, "Bear with each other and forgive whatever grievances you may have against one another. Forgive as the Lord forgave you" (Col. 3:13). If we forgive ourselves, God will forgive us. Mark 11:25-26 says, "And when you stand praying, if you hold anything against anyone, forgive him, so that your Father in Heaven may forgive you your sins: But if you do not forgive, neither will your father who is in Heaven forgive you your sins".

7. Lead Us Not into Temptation but Deliver Us from Evil (Matt. 6:13)

Trials and hurdles will always be encountered along the Christian journey. To become a finisher, you will need to overcome these challenges. This prayer is a plea for help for Christians (1 Cor. 10:13). Experiencing the hurdle is not what is feared in this prayer but giving up on it. Furthermore, the prayer pleads to be delivered from "evil" or the evil one, which is the devil or satan. God in his wisdom may allow those trials to come our way to test us in order to strengthen and prove our faithfulness to him, while satan tempts us to put us down and destroy us.

What the Bible Says:

2 Peter 2:7, 9

He rescued Lot, a righteous man who was distressed by the filthy lives of lawless men. If this is so, then the Lord knows how to rescue godly men from trials.

1 Corinthians 10:13

No temptation has seized you except what is common to man. And God is faithful; he will not let you be tempted beyond what you can bear. But when you are tempted, he will also provide a way out so that you can stand up under it.

James 1:2

Consider it pure joy, my brothers, whenever you face trials of major kinds.

James 1:13-14

When tempted, no one should say, "God is tempting me". For God cannot be tempted by evil, nor does he tempt anyone, but each one is tempted when he is dragged away by his own evil desire and enticed.

8. For the Kingdom, the Power and the Glory are Yours Now and Forever

This is an affirmation that Jesus Christ is Lord overall. He will reign forever and his kingdom will never end (Luke 1:33). His throne was established long ago and he is from all eternity (Ps. 93:2). Yours O LORD is the greatness and the power and the glory and the majesty and the splendor, for everything in heaven is yours. Yours O LORD is the Kingdom, you are exalted, a head overall (1 Chron. 29:11). If God is for us, who can be against us? (Rom. 8:31). Christians are fully protected and are under his compass. John 10:29 says, "My Father who has given them to me, is greater than all; no one can snatch them out of my Father's hand". The God we serve is able to save us (Dan. 3:17). 1 John 4:4 says, "The one who is in you is greater than the one who is in the world".

9. Amen

Amen signifies the conclusion of a prayer or a hymn and it is said at the end of a prayer or hymn meaning "so be it". Amen is a Hebrew word meaning truth, certainty. It demonstrates whole hearted commitment to what has been said in the case of prayer and in the case of a song, what has been sung. Jesus Christ is the source of power of "Amen" because he is the "Yes of all God's promises" and this in turn provides the confidence in the use of "Amen". 2 Corinthians 1:20 says, "For no matter how many promises God has made, they are "Yes" in Christ". And so through him the "Amen" is spoken by us to the glory of God. "Amen" is also used as name for Christ. In Revelation 3:14, Christ is called "the Amen" in the letter to Laodicea. In Isaiah 65:16, God is described twice as "the God of truth" (the God of Amen). The significance of the "Amen" is also noticed in the instruction of Moses to the people of Israel (Deut. 27:14-26). The "Amen" has been used as a concluding endorsement of the book of Galatians (Gal. 6:18), the book of Jude (Jude 25) and the book of Revelation (Rev. 22:21). In worship "Amen" is used as affirmative response of gratefulness to God (1 Chron. 16:36; Ps. 41:13).

What Does the Bible Say?

1 Kings 1:36

Benaiah son of Jehoiada answered the king "Amen". May the LORD, the God of my Lord the king, so declare it.

Jeremiah 11:5

Then I will fulfill the oath I swore to you forefathers, to give them a land with milk and honey – the land you possess today. I answered "Amen, LORD".

Revelation 1:7

Look, he is coming with the clouds, and every eye will see him, even those who pierced him; and all the people of the earth will mourn because of him. So shall it be Amen.

Galatians 6:18

The grace of our Lord Jesus Christ be with your spirit, brothers Amen.

Jude 25

To the only God our saviour be the glory, majesty, power and authority, through Jesus Christ our Lord, before all ages, now and forevermore Amen.

Revelation 22:21

The grace of the Lord Jesus be with God's people Amen.

1 Chronicles 16:36

Praise be to the LORD, the God of Israel, from everlasting to everlasting. Then all the people said "Amen" and "Praise the LORD."

Psalm 41:13

Praise be to the LORD, the God of Israel, from everlasting to everlasting Amen and Amen.

Galatians 1:5

To whom be glory forever and ever. Amen.

Ephesians 3:21

To him be glory in the church and in Christ Jesus throughout all generations, for ever and ever. Amen.

Chapter 21

MEDITATION SCRIPTURES BEFORE AND AFTER THE LAST SUPPER

The Last Supper

Jesus had a final meal with his disciples before the day of his crucifixion which is remembered as the 'Last Supper'. He offered bread and wine as symbols of his body and his blood in order to remember his sacrifice for us on the cross for our sins. On the night he was betrayed, while they were eating Jesus took bread, gave thanks and broke it and gave it to his disciples saying, "Take and eat, this is my body". Then he took the cup, gave thanks and offered it to them, saying, "Drink from it, all of you. This is my blood of the covenant, which is poured out for many for the forgiveness of sins. I tell you, I will not drink of this fruit of the wine from now on until that day when I drink anew with you in my Father's Kingdom" (Matthew 26:26-29).

Other Names for the Last Supper

The Lord's Supper is also served under various names:

1. Eucharist – Greek word for 'thanks', (Matt. 26:27; 1 Cor. 11:24)
2. The breaking of bread (Acts 2:42, 46; 20:7)
3. Communion (1 Cor. 10:16 KJV)
4. The Lord's table (1 Cor. 10:21)
5. The Lord's supper (1 Cor. 11:20)
6. Love feast (Jude 12).

Some churches serve the Last Supper weekly or monthly.

Meditation Scriptures Before the "Last Supper"

- *Let us examine our ways and test them, and let us return to the Lord (Lamentation 3:40).*
- *Test me O LORD and try me, examine my heart and my mind (Psalm 26:2).*
- *I have considered my ways and have turned my steps to your status. I will hasten and not delay to obey your commands (Psalm 119:59-60).*
- *For whenever you eat this bread and drink this cup, you proclaim the Lord's death until he comes. A man ought to examine himself before he eats of the bread and drinks of the cup (1 Corinthians 11:26, 28).*
- *Get rid of the old yeast that you may be a new batch without yeast – as you really are. For Christ, our Passover Lamb has been sacrificed. Therefore, let us keep the Festival, not with the old yeast, the yeast of malice and wickedness, but with bread without yeast, the bread of sincerity and truth (I Corinthians 5:7-8).*
- *I am the living bread that came from Heaven. If anyone eats of this bread, he will live forever. This bread is my flesh, which I will give for the life of the world (John 6:51).*
- *Jesus said to them, "I tell you the truth, unless you can eat the flesh of the son of man and drink his blood, you have no life in you. Whoever eats my flesh and drinks my blood has eternal life, and I will raise him up at the last day. For my flesh is real food and my blood is real drink. Whoever eats my flesh and drinks my blood remains in me, and I in him. Just as the living Father sent me and I live because of the Father, so the one who feeds on me will live because of me. This is the bread that came down from heaven. Your forefathers ate manna and died, but he who feeds on this bread will live forever" (John 6:53-58).*
- *This is my blood of the covenant, which is poured out for many, he said to them (Mark 14:24).*
- *If we confess our sins, he is faithful and just and will forgive us our sins and purify us from all unrighteousness (1 John 1:19).*

- *My dear children, I write this to you so that you will not sin. But if anyone does sin, we have one who speaks to the Father in our defense. Jesus Christ, the Righteous one (1 John 2:1).*
- *Therefore, brothers, since we have confidence to enter the Most Holy Place by the blood of Jesus, by a new and living way opened for us through the curtain, that is, his body, and since we have a great priest over the house of God, let us draw near to God with a sincere heart in full assurance of faith (Heb. 10:19-22).*

Meditation Scriptures After the 'Last Supper'

- *He withdrew about a stone's throw beyond them. Knelt down and prayed. Father, if you are willing, take this cup from me, yet not my will but yours be done. And being in anguish, he prayed more earnestly, and his sweat was like drops of blood falling to the ground (Luke 22:41-42, 44).*
- *But he was pierced for our transgressions, he was crushed for our iniquities, the punishment that brought us peace was upon him, and by his wounds we are healed (Isaiah 53:5).*
- *Finally Pilate handed him over to them to be crucified. So the soldiers took charge of Jesus. Carrying his own cross, he went out to the Place of the Skull (which in Aramaic is called Golgotha). Here, they crucified him (John 19:16-18).*
- *One of the soldiers pierced Jesus' side with a spear, bringing a sudden flow of blood and water (John 19:34).*
- *For the life of a creature is in the blood, and I have given it to you to make atonement for yourselves on the altar; it is the blood that makes atonement for one's life (Leviticus 17:11).*
- *It is impossible for the blood of bulls and goats to take away sins (Hebrews 10:4).*
- *He did not enter by means of the blood of goats and calves; but he entered the Most Holy Place once for all by his own blood, having obtained eternal redemption (Hebrews 9:12).*

- *And through him to reconcile to himself all things, whether things on Earth or things in Heaven, by making peace through his blood, shed on the cross (**Colossians 1:20**).*
- *For you know that it was not with perishable things such as silver or gold that you were redeemed from the empty way of life handed down to you from your forefathers, but with the precious blood of Christ, a lamb without blemish or defect (1 Peter 1:18-19).*

Chapter 22

GOSPEL OF GRACE (1): MY UPBRINGING

❈

In Psalm 113:7-8, the Psalmist says, "He raises the poor from the dust and lifts the needy from the ash heap: he seats them with princes: with princes of their people". This is exactly what I experienced in my life as my testimony explains. I was not born into a wealthy family. My father, Alfred, was a fisherman and our livelihood was dependent on subsistence fishing which barely provided necessities for our daily living. I never thought of advancing in my educational career beyond what my dad could afford. He did not have the extra to pay for the luxury of sending me to a grammar school. He was not educated. He could neither read nor write but he was very passionate about education. He never wanted me to become a fisherman, although he made me a little fishing net just to acquaint me with the Ijaw culture and occupation. He was very kind and loving. He enrolled me in the village school to start with preparatory primary education. Later I advanced to the lower primary level. Quite surprisingly, an opportunity occurred to serve as a house boy. My dad asked me to go and serve my uncle, Gideon Iringe-Koko, a teacher at St. Martins School, Ogu in Okrika district then. I was quite a little boy but I was very enthusiastic for the opportunity to serve him. I travelled with him to Ogu town to start a new life. It was quite difficult learning to cope with helping my uncle and without my dad around me. God helped me and I was able to settle quite quickly. After a few years, my uncle was transferred to another school at Kugbo (St. Michaels's school, Kugbo) as the headmaster. In those days, Kugbo town was quite a distant place to access.

When travelling to Kugbo, we went through Abonnema town where we took a canoe with paddlers who paddled day and night for two days through the creeks and water ways surrounded by thick forests and mangroves. It was a difficult and frightening experience. As a little boy, it was quite an experience. I commend the inhabitants of Kugbo. They were really kind and loving which indeed reduced the fear of the unknown in an environment considered very far from home and not easily accessible. God finally saw us through. Unfortunately, the school stopped at primary 5 level. When I completed the primary 5 class, my uncle made an alternative arrangement for me to return back to St. Martins school Ogu to complete my primary school education.

When I was leaving him, he advised that I should not sit for the entrance examination into any secondary school be it a grammar school or government college because they were quite expensive and beyond affordability of a teacher. My dad was in support of my uncle's position because he told me that secondary school education was for the rich and not for poor people. My uncle advised that instead after my primary school education, I should sit for the entrance examination into any of the teachers' training schools where no fees were charged but instead allowances were paid to students. I accepted that advice but least did I know that God had another plan for me.

When admission forms into the secondary schools both for grammar schools and Government Colleges were received by the school in 1956, the headmaster invited me to see him in his office. When I visited him he informed me that he had prepared the list of scholars to sit for the common entrance examination into the secondary schools and my name was on the list. He also informed me that the examination fee was three shillings. I told him that my uncle and my dad said I should not sit for the examination into secondary schools because my uncle could not afford secondary school fees. These schools were for the rich and not for the poor. He insisted that as one of the brightest children in the class, the school could not afford to leave my name out because they wanted to promote the image of the school. He said he would delay sending out the forms and the list for a while to give me time to source for the three shillings fee. I left his office quite confused, because I could not go against what the headmaster had said. After a couple of weeks, he sent for me and informed me that he had sent out the forms and the list to the general manger of schools office in Port-Harcourt, and that my fees were paid and I should reimburse the school. I thanked him and refunded the fees in bits.

The next hurdle was how to pay for my transport fare from Ogu to Port-Harcourt for the entrance examination because St. Cyprian's school Port-Harcourt was the center for the entrance examination. The fare for an engine boat transport from Ogu to Port-Harcourt was one shilling and six pence. I did not have the money. When some of my classmates visited to check on me, I was crying and informed them that I was not travelling for the examination because I did not have the money to pay for transport fare. They were worried. They loved me so much and could go any length for my sake. They met and changed to plan B. They came back and informed me that to help me, they had changed their plan. They said instead of going by engine boat transport, they had decided to go by foot through the land to Port-Harcourt. On the eve of the day to the entrance examination, we left at 6pm in the evening on barefoot. We trekked through forests, bushes and farmlands and arrived in Port-Harcourt at about 7:30am in the morning the next day meaning that we trekked for thirteen and half hours throughout the night. God protected us from dangerous snakes and animals. As soon as we arrived Port-Harcourt, I washed my face in a friend's father's house and went straight to St. Mary's church to pray. When I returned I bought some food to eat and later joined my class mates to the examination hall at St. Cyprian's school Port-Harcourt.

After the entrance examination, I took the opportunity to visit my town, Amadi-Ama, Ogoloma as it is one of the closest Okrika villages to Port-Harcourt to see my father. He was quite surprised to see me. I told him that I came to Port-Harcourt to sit for the common entrance examination to grammar schools and Government Colleges. He was shocked and said to me that my uncle would not be happy with my action because these schools were for the rich and not for the poor. I told him that I could not help it because the headmaster forced me into it. I told him I was sorry. I had to return back to Ogu with the money I collected from him to pay for engine boat fare back to Ogu. As soon as I sat for the primary 6 level final examination, I returned back to my town. While in my town, I received the news that I was successful in the common entrance examination into secondary schools. I thanked God and went straight to inform my dad of the good news. He told me that since my uncle did not have the money for a secondary school education, there was nothing he could do. I wept bitterly. My dad got worried because I never stopped weeping for some days. When my uncle arrived for the 1956 Christmas holiday, my dad welcomed him and informed him that I had passed the common entrance examination to grammar school. Instead of getting angry, my uncle was excited. He immediately sent for me. I ran to him and he exclaimed, so you passed the entrance to grammar school? I said yes. Then he said to me, you have done your part and by the Grace of God he would do his part. He said again, that I should start preparing for surely I would attend the grammar school. I started in January 1957. Thank God in my second year, I got a council scholarship which reduced the burden on my uncle.

I finished in December 1961. In 1962 I got admission into school of Agriculture Umudike, Umuahia. I started in January 1963. While studying, the government still paid us our full Cambridge school certificate salaries. I was included in the school football team. The change in my economic status, my youthful age, and exposure to wider society made me fall short of my commitment to the Lord. I read the Bible randomly and I could count the days I went to worship in the church. I developed a casual approach to things of God. My faith was still focused but my actions were not matching. After school of agriculture, I had a brief spell in the ministry of agriculture. The civil war started in 1967 and I was caught up in it. I called on the Lord and he picked me up again. He helped me escape to my town. At the end of the civil war I got a scholarship to study accountancy in the UK. I also got married to my wife, Grace. I teamed up with her to rededicate our lives back to God. What I never expected in my life, he made it possible for me. He gave me one of the best education and some of the best jobs. In OPEC officers from member countries are automatically given diplomatic status by the Austrian government. My family members and I enjoyed full diplomatic privileges throughout my 8 years service. Presently, the Nigeria LNG, a company I contributed to the success story, is the most successful company in Nigeria. Amazingly, the head office is located within my village Amadi-ama, Port-harcourt. These are unmerited favour from God. What an amazing grace indeed.

From my personal experience, Jesus accepts us unconditionally, just as we are, regardless of our background. He sees something good in everyone. Remember that how Christ sees you is of greater importance than how others do or how you see yourself. Christ sees your potential. He sees your destiny and knows what you can become when you are prepared to put your complete trust in him. Invite him into your life and your future will be better than your past. Romans 9:33 says, "The one who trusts in him will never be put to shame".

Chapter 23

GOSPEL OF GRACE (2):
MY COVID-19 EXPERIENCE

---- ✳ ----

My covid-19 experience can be divided into three parts:

1). Decision to Move Out Of Abuja In 2018
2). Decision to Cancel My Plan to Travel to London for the 2019 Christmas
3). Decision to travel to London in March 2021

The Holy Spirit is God's presence in our midst (John 16:13-15). My covid-19 experience is a glaring example and testimony of the important role the Holy Spirit plays in the life of believers. The part played by the Spirit may not be clear to us at the beginning but at the end it will become evident and may sound mysterious. The Holy Spirit is our counsellor, our helper, and our guide (John 16:7-15). John 16:13 says, "When he the Spirit of truth comes, he will guide you into all truth. He will not speak on his own, he will speak only what he hears, and he will tell you what is yet to come". In the three decisions that I took, I acted as if I knew what was coming in future but that was not the case. I took the three decisions like a robot without considering the risks and weighing the options. At the end, I discovered that the counsellor and our guide was at work in me.

The Lord is indeed a good refuge in times of trouble. He cares for those who put their trust in him. He is a personal, caring and loving God. In John 16:33 Jesus said, "In the world you will have trouble. But take heart! I have overcome the world". No matter how frightening things may be, Jesus is still in control. Through his death on the cross he rose to life again. He overcame death and defeated the devil. We will go through the storm of life but will not be defeated or consumed. In the end, believers will be victorious. From my covid-19 experiences, God sees beyond our present circumstances. There is nothing that happens that God does not directly or indirectly permit. God will take us out of the storm or he will certainly lead us safely through it. In my case, he partly took me out of the covid-19 heat and also led me through the moderate path when vaccines became available. My testimony tells it all.

1. Decision to Move Out Of Abuja In 2018

I started living in Abuja since 1999. My plan was to move out of Abuja in 2025 to my village as my final retirement home. Surprisingly in May 2018, I decided suddenly to return to my village without considering whether it was a wise decision or not despite the fact that it was a life changing decision. I left my village since 1971 and for over 51 years, I have never lived on average up to four weeks in a year in my village. The fact that I did not visit my village regularly did not mean that I was out of touch. I loved my village because that is my root. I regularly spent my annual leave every year in my village. During family emergencies and when work exigencies are minimal, I took casual leave to travel to the village. Throughout my working life, I never lost sight of my root.

The decision to move out of Abuja in May 2018 was taken and on the same day I started packing my belongings. I did not make consultations. I called on my landlord and settled whatever was needed to be settled in respect of moving out of my flat at short notice. When the truck was ready to leave the flat, I contacted my children that I was leaving Abuja to the village, Amadi-Ama an Ogoloma town in Okrika North Archdeaconry in Port-Harcourt Local Government. My children were shocked on hearing the news. I could not explain the whys. I did things like a robot.

Electricity supply in my village was the greatest challenge that would have made me change my mind if I had the time to think about moving out of my Abuja residence. Although my village is located in Port-Harcourt, it is confronted with poor electricity supply. That would have meant my generator would be on constant usage and that would affect my affordability. But fortunately, I never thought of all these obstacles. I left Abuja on a Saturday morning flight on the 12th of May 2018. I arrived in my village at about 11:00am. There was no light and I was informed that for the past few days there had not been light in the village. It was then I remembered that I did not put electricity supply into consideration before I made my decision. I was trying to feel some despair but surprisingly, by 12:30pm, light came into the house. I was so thankful to God.

Settling into a completely new life was quite challenging. However, the village environment was more relaxing. In the process of settling down, the covid-19 virus struck Nigeria in February 2020. When I heard the news I then recollected that the decision to pack out of Abuja was not mine but God's decision. Abuja is the second epic center, next to Lagos. My flat in Abuja was such that I could not have been able to isolate. Even the environment itself would have exposed me to the infection. In my village, I was able to keep indoors and had space to self-isolate and have some exercise and also sit in the garden and relax in the sun.

2. Decision to Cancel My Plan to Travel to London for the 2019 Christmas

My children live in England and for the past 20 years I never missed spending the Christmas with them in England. The Hillsong Christmas carol is my very favourite Christmas event. I always cherished and looked forward to attending every year. In the summer of 2019, while I was with them in London, I informed them that I would skip the 2019 Christmas in London and would not be travelling to join them for Christmas. Furthermore I would not be attending the Hillsong Christmas carol. At the time I was passing this information I could not understand or explain the whys. There was sadness all over everyone due to the news. I returned to Nigeria on 17 July 2019. I bought the essential things I needed since I would not return to London soon. Truly and surprisingly, I spent the Christmas in my village without the children being around. Later on, events started unfolding. The coronavirus pandemic was reported in December 2019 in China. Early in January 2020, it was reported in Europe and in the UK. Nigeria experienced its first index case in February 2020. Report carried it that people of my age (over 70s) were at higher risk of surviving the pandemic infection. The impact of the pandemic was more serious on those who travelled outside the country (Nigeria) late in 2019 and returned early in 2020 when not much was known about the disease. When I recollected that those periods were within the months I usually travelled to London to spend the Christmas with my family, I burst into joy and started praising and thanking God for stopping me from travelling to London for the 2019 Christmas. Some concerned friends called to know where I was when the pandemic struck. They relaxed when they heard I never travelled to London and furthermore I was in my village and not in Abuja. Some said I was lucky while some said "God loves you". I finally realised that all my actions and decisions not to travel for the Christmas were all promptings from the Holy Spirit because he knew what was coming in the future. The Holy Spirit is Christ in our midst. John 16:13 says, "When the Spirit of truth comes, he will guide you into all truth. He will not speak on his own; he will speak only what he hears, and he will tell you what is yet to come". Hallelujah.

3. Decision to Travel to London in March 2021

After a long wait of about 18 months and finally being in desperate need, I decided early in March 2021 to travel to London to join my family. But this time around, International travelling has been made more difficult due to the pandemic. All persons travelling to the UK were expected to meet all governmental covid-19 requirements to help stop the spread. In summary, the hurdles included a proof of a negative covid-19 test taken within 3 days of departure to the UK. All arrivals must take a coronavirus test on days 2 and 8 of their quarantine period. I thank God that Nigeria was excluded from the red list countries and I did not need to book a quarantine hotel on arrival. About the time I travelled (early March 2021), travelling, especially international travel, was still as risky and dangerous as before. The only difference was that better steps were taken by the governments and airlines to protect travelers from the spread of coronavirus.

Unlike before, this time around I had a very strong feeling to travel, which meant it was God's approved time for me to travel. My air ticket which I booked over months ago was now confirmed for 7 March 2021. The journey commenced from Port-Harcourt, South-South Nigeria on 6 March 2021 to Abuja, Federal Capital City of Nigeria. My covid-19 test in Nigeria was negative which gave me the green light to travel. On 7 March 2021, I proceeded to the Nnamdi Azikiwe International Airport Abuja in the morning to board the British Airways flight to London Heathrow. I checked in my luggage and collected my boarding pass. When the departure (boarding) was announced, I proceeded to board the plane. When I boarded, I decided to change the seat on my boarding pass. My boarding pass was having a window seat but I decided to seek for permission to change to a seat in the middle of the plane far from my original seat. My request for change was granted and I made the change. Events later turned out that it was a wise and life-saving decision inspired by God.

The plane took off at about 9am from Abuja and arrived at the London Heathrow at about 4.40pm. I successfully went through the covid-19 protocols. I was picked up at the airport. I arrived at the house safely with great excitement and relief. Hallelujah. The worries and challenges of the journey, the later developments that followed and my trust in the Lord to make it were inspired by my meditation on some scripture passages especially Isaiah 43:2-3 and Psalm 23:4. My quarantine commenced as I got to the house. After two days of quarantine, I had my day 2 covid-19 test and the result was negative. Hallelujah.

While I was hoping, praying and looking forward that the day 8 covid-19 test should also come with a negative result, quite surprisingly and shocking I received a worrisome email message on 12th March 2021 from the Public Health England that a passenger who sat in close proximity to me on the same flight had tested positive for covd-19 and that I was at a high risk of being infected with the virus. I must therefore quarantine for 10 days. Part of the message read, "Dear Mr. Iringe-Koko, the International Travel Contact Tracing Team of Public Health England has been informed of a person who travelled on the same flight as you arriving on 07/03/2021 who has contracted the covid-19 virus. We understand that you were in close proximity to the person and at increased risk of catching the virus. You must therefore quarantine for 10 days after arrival date of the flight 07/03/2021". I panicked after reading through the message a couple of times. I meditated several times on my favourite scripture passages as if I was starting a second journey. In the midst of the confusion I said to myself hold on a minute. I started retracing and retracking my steps at the time I boarded the flight. I then recollected that I rejected the seat on my boarding pass and changed to a different seat from my original seat on the boarding pass. I breathed a sigh of relief. But unfortunately it was not over yet because I needed to go through the day 8 covid-19 test for full assurance that I did not sit close to the covid-19 positive passenger. I did the test on 19 March 2021. The result was negative and I regained my freedom after 10 days quarantine, Hallelujah. It was a journey in the midst of life and death. I travelled through three airports, especially considering that London Heathrow International Airport is one of the busiest airports in the world. To add to that, I was presumed to have sat in close proximity to a passenger on the same flight who tested positive for coid-19. The journey involved three covid-19 tests, one in Nigeria and two in the UK and all of them were negative. What an amazing grace! A favour which I least merited. Hallelujah.

I encourage believers to share their experiences and testimonies on how the gospel of grace has touched their lives. Such testimonies promote the work of the ministry. In the

New Testament, Christ wants believers to share their experiences on how the Lord is good. In Mark 5:19 Jesus asked the demon possessed man after healing him, "Go home to your family and tell them how much the Lord has done for you". In Acts 4:19-20, when the leaders of the Jews wanted Peter and John not to share their testimonies about Jesus' miracles, they answered, "Judge for yourselves whether it is right in God's sight to obey you rather than God. For we cannot help speaking about what we have seen and heard". Praise God.

Chapter 24

COVID-19 PANDEMIC AND
THE LESSONS

1. Brief Reflection on Covid-19 Pandemic

Covid-19 pandemic was an unprecedented outbreak that shook the world. Before covid-19 struck, the world was in high spirit. The year 2020 was predicted with all certainty as a great year. But after a few weeks covid-19 pandemic struck. The world was turned upside down. The pandemic changed world issues. There has been nothing quite as usual and affecting almost all parts of the world. It was an unprecedented outbreak that put much of the world under lockdown. Nations were confronted with the biggest economic crisis and worst public health crises. Landmark events such as the Olympic Games were cancelled or postponed. Covid-19 was a devastating strike that has changed the rules of globalisation and human effort in solving problems of human nature. There has been nothing quite as universal with such a devastating effect. People were forced out of their comfort zones. The economy, travel industry and people's mental health have all taken a battering. Worship places were not spared. They were shadows of themselves. Evangelism and crusade events could hardly function because of lockdowns and restrictions on mass gathering. Hallelujah, Covid-19 vaccines are now available, although not universally. The good news has brought relief and hope to the world. Nations are now eager to start a new normal life, to restart the economy, improve mental health, and get the world socialising again, but the lessons of the covid-19 pandemic must not be forgotten too soon.

2. The Modern World and the Spiritual Aspect of Covid-19 Pandemic Storm

The covid-19 pandemic is a typical example of storms of life. In the Book of Exodus, God sent plagues to Egypt to restrain and humble Pharaoh for his disobedience. The 40 years journey through the wilderness was to humble the Israelites (Deut. 8:2). He is the everlasting God, who sits enthroned on high, who stoops down to look on the Heavens and the earth (Psalm 113:5-6). He does as he pleases with the powers of Heaven and the people of the Earth. No one can hold back his hand or say to him, what have you done? (Dan. 4:35). He created the Earth, sustains the Earth day and night (24/7) and never grows tired (Isa. 40:28). Thus there is no storm that he does not directly or indirectly approve. The covid-19 pandemic storm is not different. To continue with the narrative, I would like to reflect on how Christianity has fared in the modern society.

3. Christianity and the New World

Christianity in terms of publicity has fared better, mostly due to improved communication technology. Church worship services, messages from evangelism and crusade events are beamed and heard all over the world. However, in terms of the things of God, Christianity has not had the desired impact on the modern world which is fast sliding into materialism and ungodliness.

4. Some of the Modern World Challenges:

(i).   In the modern world, preaching of sin has become an inconvenience. The message of the cross which is central to the Bible plan has also been watered down due to the drive for patronage and materialism. In the modern world sin has become the most unpleasant topic to preach.

(ii).   The Bible is true, trustworthy, God breathed and a reliable rule of conduct and discipline for believers. The locus of inspiration and infallibility of the Bible is in its original manuscripts and not the translations. We cannot ignore the fact that a translation can only be reliable when it accurately reflects the meaning of the inspired originals (2 Peter 1:21). From all indications, the modern world seems to be encroaching on the interpretation of the Bible for our conduct and discipline.

(iii). The momentum generated in the past to drive the 'Focused Ministry' to reach out to the people of the world through the needy areas of society has been deflated. In the past, the church and other Christian organisations invested in schools, colleges, universities, hospitals, health centres, and low-cost hostels all over the world to promote the sharing of the Christian faith which is built on love, mercy, peace, compassion, justice, self-control, gentleness, kindness, joy, faithfulness and so on.

(iv). The lack of godliness in the modern world has also promoted the closure of churches for commercial purposes. In the past, Christian bookshops sprang up all over the world but in the modern world we have seen huge reductions in their numbers. Some have gone online and some sold out for commercial purposes.

(v). During Christmas festivals, the nativity plays to celebrate the birth of Christ were popular in the past, but they seem to be eroding in the modern world. Equally, Christmas greetings cards have virtually been transformed to season's greetings cards and the name of the saviour Jesus Christ is never mentioned. Christmas is more than season's greetings. Christmas is a time we celebrate the birth of our saviour, Jesus Christ, who is the feeling of hope in our lives, the promise of peace in the world and the blessing of God's love in our hearts. Christ is the prince of peace and our peace (Isa. 9:6; Eph. 2:14). Luke 2:13-14 says the heavenly host appeared with the angel praising God and saying, "Glory to God in the highest, and on Earth, peace to men on whom his favour rests". The world cannot understand because of living in spiritual darkness.

(vi). The modern world has also affected the teaching of the Bible in schools, colleges and institutions of higher learning. Religious studies were popular in the past but in the modern world debates are still going on whether to scrap it or not.

(vii). Materialism and ungodliness have turned the world to a modern world where there is no love, where wickedness thrives, where corruption thrives, where discrimination thrives, where inequality thrives. The modern world has become a world of 'zero sum game' (Winner takes all) without compassion, justice and mercy.

(viii). The modern world has witnessed exponential increase in the activities of false preachers, evangelists, miracle healers and prophets and so on. True believers must hold on to the faith and not give up because of those who use Christianity to fulfill their personal interests and agenda. Hold unto what you have so that no one will take your crown (Rev. 3:11). In Matthew 7:22-23, Jesus says, "Many will say to me on that day, Lord, Lord, did we not prophesy in your name and in your name drive out demons and perform many miracles? Then I will tell them plainly, I never knew you. Away from me evil doers".

The covid-19 pandemic storm generated anxiety, fear, sorrow, grief, weeping and uncertainty all over the universe as the people of the world remained helpless for a while. It was not surprising that the time was ripe for the works of power and authority in an ungodly world. God in his wisdom may permit the covid-19 storm to show that the world is living on false security, and cannot guarantee the people of the world peace without God. In John 14:27, Jesus says, "Peace I live with you; My peace I give you. I do not give to you as the world gives". Despite the fact that humans fulfill the divine image of God's creation in the book of Genesis with the command from God to fill and subdue and rule the Earth (Gen 1:26-28), God is still in control of the world forever. In Isaiah 40:25; 43:3, 10, 11, God says, "To whom will you compare me? Or who is my equal? For I am the Lord your God, the holy one of Israel, your saviour. Before me, no god was formed, nor will there be anyone after me. I, even I, am the Lord and apart from me there is no saviour".

God has a purpose for every storm. I have no doubt in my mind that God in his wisdom and whose name is Jealous (Exod. 34:14) may permit the covid-19 pandemic storm to humble the world, as he did to the Israelites in their 40 years journey through the wilderness (Deut. 8:2). Furthermore, the New Testament storm (Mark 4:35-41) is not different from the covid-19 pandemic storm. It was also for God's purpose as we will find out later.

5. The New Testament Storm and the Covid-19 Storm

In the New Testament, while the storm was ragging, Jesus was sleeping on a cushion. Despite the fact that Jesus was with the disciples, they panicked and woke him, saying to him, "Teacher, don't you care if we drown?" Jesus got up and rebuked the wind and it stopped (Mark 4:38-39). The storm in the New Testament was used to teach the disciples that Jesus is God. Before the storm, they did not understand that Jesus is God that came in human flesh. That was why they asked each other "Who is this? Even the wind and the waves obey him" (Mark 4:41). Jesus also used the storm to teach the disciples to trust him. God in his wisdom may have used the covid-19 pandemic storm to humble the world and show that human effort alone without God cannot solve all human problems. Hallelujah, covid-19 vaccines are now available, although not universally. Of course a vaccine or any form of cure was expected at some point in time because of what Apostle Paul said in 1 Cor. 10:13. The good news has brought relief and hope to the world. Countries are now eager to start a new normal life, to restart the economy, improve mental health, and get the world socialising again. In the New Testament storm the disciples of Jesus did not forget the lessons. I hope the lessons of covid-19 pandemic storm will not be forgotten soon by the world.

6. The Fall of Man and Covid-19 Pandemic

Before Adam sinned, there was a perfect relationship that existed between him and God. This cordial relationship made him completely dependent on God. He did not need to worry for food, there was security for him and he did not have to worry about tomorrow and what will happen. He was totally secured. He and his wife, Eve, were both naked but they felt no shame. God covered their nakedness. His disobedience and the desire to be like God exposed their nakedness, meaning that he was nothing without God. Their eyes opened when they noticed their nakedness and shame engulfed them. Adam and his wife have to labour for their living; they have to live in fear, uncertainty and shame. The Adam situation is not different from what the world experienced during the covid-19 pandemic. The world experienced a level of unprecedented nakedness, emptiness, helplessness, uncertainty, fear and incompleteness. All these were signs that something supernatural was missing. In the book of Genesis, God for his love for humanity commanded humans he created in his image to take charge of his creation, subdue and have dominion over his creation (Gen. 1:26-28). But that does not give human the divine authority to take over from God, who is the king eternal, immortal, invisible, the only God (1 Tim. 1:17). In a world that is fast sliding towards materialism and ungodly desires, God may in his wisdom directly or indirectly permit the covid-19 pandemic storm to humble the world, test our faith and character. The pandemic was unusual and nothing quite as universal which reflects what God said in Jeremiah 23:24, "Can anyone hide in secret places so that I cannot see him? Do not I fill Heaven and Earth?" The world may not understand because of being in spiritual darkness. Adam brought darkness to the world. Jesus brought light to the world. Through Christ, Christians are the light of the world. If the world cannot understand because of being in spiritual darkness, Christians are supposed to fill the vacuum (Matt. 5:13-16). They must shine until darkness departs. Christianity is about change. Christianity ended the primitive way of life in Africa. Christianity brought an end to slave trade.

7. The Pandemic May Have Been Used to Demonstrate God's Love and Justice

The foundation of God's throne is built on righteousness and justice (Ps. 97:2). God loves justice and acts with justice (Ps. 33:5). This was demonstrated during the pandemic. To discuss this topic further, I want to first reflect on some of the instances where God demonstrated his justice. God's love never conflicts with his justice. This was demonstrated in his saving activity. Because of God's love for us, he gave his only son for us as a sacrificial lamb, and because of his justice, Christ died for our sins on the cross to make us stand justified before God (1 Tim. 2:5-6). His justice is also demonstrated in the punishment of Israel for their disobedience and rebellion in the wilderness. Those who were 20 years and over were presumed to be well informed of God's signs and wonders in Egypt. For this group of people, God denied them entry into the Promised Land (Canaan). Apart from Joshua and Caleb that were spared, the rest perished in the wilderness. Those under 20 years of age and the ones born during the 40 years journey in the wilderness were presumed innocent. God granted them entry into the Promised Land, thereby demonstrating his love and justice (Num. 14:26-38). God is the same yesterday, the same today and the same forever.

The same pattern of delivering justice was repeated during the pandemic. It is universally acknowledged that babies, children and the young people were spared of catching covid-19 infection. If any, infections among the young were very moderate or mild. There was also great concern that African countries would experience very serious covid-19 related deaths due to lack of medical facilities, medicines, and vaccine discrimination. It was also feared that the roads could be littered with covid-19 deaths, but this did not happen because of his justice, love, mercy and compassion. God's justice is also captured in 2 Peter 2:4-9. It says, "For if God did not spare angels when they sinned but sent them to hell, putting them into gloomy dungeons to be held for judgment; if he did not spare the ancient world when he brought the flood on its ungodly people, but protected Noah, a

159

preacher of righteousness and seven others; if he condemned the cities of Sodom and Gomorrah by burning them to ashes, and made them an example of what is going to happen to the ungodly; and if he rescued Lot, a righteous man, who was distressed by the filthy lives of the lawless men (for that righteous man, living among them day after day, was tormented in his righteous soul by the lawless deeds he saw and heard). If this is so, then the Lord knows how to rescue godly men from trials and to hold the unrighteous for the day of judgment while continuing their punishment".

From what the Bible says, pandemic cannot be unexpected in an ungodly world. In Psalm14:2-3, the Psalmist says, "The LORD looks down from heaven on the sons of men to see if there are any who seek God. All have turned aside; they have together become corrupt; there is no one who does good, not even one". God created the world and he is in firm control. There is nothing that happens that is outside his knowledge. He directly or indirectly approves everything. He may not have directly brought the pandemic upon us. However in a modern world where wickedness and ungodliness thrive, the devil may have caused the pandemic and God who reigns in righteousness and justice may have given his approval directly or indirectly as a warning for the world to seek repentance and forgiveness. We should always have in mind what Apostle Paul says in his letter in 1 Corinthians 10:13, "No temptation has seized you except what is common to man. And God is faithful; he will not let you be tempted beyond what you can bear. But when you are tempted, he will also provide a way out so that you can stand up under it". Vaccines and varieties of drugs are now available to deal with covid-19 infections. In parts of Africa, local herbs are known to deal with covid-19 illness. In most part of the world, health personnel have acquired the experience to deal with covid-19 patients and prevention. New health facilities have become available in dealing with covid-19 related patients. God's patience allows people to come to repentance and come back to him. He is patient with us, not wanting anyone to perish, but everyone to come to repentance. In the case of sinful people of Nineveh, God's patience led them to repentance. In Jonah 3:9-10, the king of Nineveh said, "Who knows? God may yet relent and with compassion turn from his fierce anger so that we will not perish. When God saw what they did and how they turned from their evil ways, he had compassion and did not bring upon them the destruction he had threatened". Also the forty years of disobedience of the Israelites in the desert (Acts 13:18) show that God is patient for a long time with sinful people. He endured their misconduct for forty years.

The Lessons

Jesus gave us the key to survival during storms of life. If we built our house on solid rock instead of sand, we will survive any storm. The rock is Jesus. People who trust in Jesus will survive when the storm comes. Our faith and trust in the Lord Jesus bring him on board with us. When we trust him and put our faith in him, there is certainty, peace, comfort and assurance in the midst of storms of life. He assures us of safe landing. We will make it to the other side (Mark 5:1). You do not need to worry about drowning. Is Jesus in your boat? Have you invited him into your life? The disciples did not forget the lessons of the storm in the New Testament. The people of the world must not forget the lessons of covid-19 pandemic.

The Word of Spirit and of Power

Mathew 25:13

Therefore keep watch, because you do not know the day or the hour.

Luke 21:34-35

Be careful or your hearts will be weighed down with dissipation, drunkenness and the anxieties of life, and that day will close on you unexpectedly like a trap. For it will come upon all those who live on the face of the whole Earth.

1 Thessalonians 5:2-4

For you know very well that the day of the Lord will come like a thief in the night. While people are saying "peace and safety", destruction will come on them suddenly, as labour pains on a pregnant woman, and they will not escape. But you, brothers, are not in darkness so that this day should surprise you like a thief.

Psalm 78: 38-39

Yet he was merciful; he forgave their iniquities and did not destroy them. Time after time he restrained his anger and did not stir up his full wrath. He remembered that they were but flesh, a passing breeze that does not return.

Psalm 103:8-10

The Lord is compassionate and gracious, slow to anger, abounding in love. He will not always accuse, nor will he harbour his anger forever, he does not treat us as our sins deserve or repay us according to our iniquities.

Jonah 4:2

You are a gracious and compassionate God, slow to anger and abounding in love, a God who relents from sending calamity.

Jeremiah 14:7, 20

Although our sins testify against us, O LORD, do something for the sake of your name. For our backsliding is great; we have sinned against you. O LORD we acknowledge our wickedness and the guilt of our fathers; we have indeed sinned against you.

Chapter 25

MAKING LIFE-CHANGING DECISIONS

Seek God's Wisdom and Guidance

Some examples of life changing decisions include: marriage, divorce, taking up mortgage, change of employment, terminating employment of a staff, going into politics, changing a career, abandoning the faith, relocating to a foreign country and so on. Seek God's wisdom always in making life changing decisions. Follow King Solomon's example (1 Kings 3:9-14).

Godly wisdom is wise living. Develop the capacity to look at decisions based on God's viewpoint. We only know what humans can know. God knows yesterday, today and the future. God has never said I have forgotten something. Whenever we are walking with God, we can go through the deepest and darkest part of life. Prayer is God's appointed way to get what we need. Be careful. Decisions made out of fear, anxiety or worry are susceptible to being wrong. Make every thought obedient to God.

Be Patient and Read the Bible

Be patient. Don't be rushed into taking life-changing decisions. Most life-changing decisions can hardly be reversed. Stay in the 'Word' for your decisions. Reference the 'Word' of God in the Bible to ensure that your decisions tie into what the 'Word' says. What we read and what we listen to, feed the soul. The 'Word' of God helps you take decisions (Heb. 4:12-13). God speaks to believers through his "Word" (the Bible). The more you read the Bible, the more the "Word" becomes part of you and the more you walk closer to God (John 15:7). Make up your mind to set aside time to read the Bible daily and not just randomly. There is so much power in God's "Word" and that is all you need to make wise decisions. The Bible is not a book we can sideline for a while. It is one of the greatest resources that believers have but unfortunately it has been under-utilised. What you need for your marriage, financial life, career, children and so on are all in the Bible.

Put Aside Selfish Desires

With God you can overcome your selfish desires and your old self in making decisions. Decisions taken based on what can make you happy will fail. Worldly desires can affect taking wise decisions because such desires can override God's will in your life. Always ask is this the right thing to do? Godly wisdom is wise living.

Check the Circumstances Around

What is happening to the economy, employment market, the political environment, the annual budget, government policies? Evaluate what impact these could make on your decisions. Seek advice or counsel from mature believers who had walked that path before. Check and seek advice or counseling from your church council. Decisions are about having good judgment through the ability to undertake proper analysis of what is right and wrong and allowing the Holy Spirit to direct your actions. Finally, decisions should be based on what is right and not what it will cost us to do what is right.

My Experience in Making a Life-changing Decision

The very day I started my new assignment in Nigeria after my overseas duty tour, I was faced with the directive to sack a staff in my department whom I have never seen or worked with. It was one of the greatest challenges I encountered in my life. It was glaring that if I did not implement the directive to sack the staff,

I would be in direct collision with the powers that are in authority. The directive was to be implemented immediately considering that the salary of the staff had been stopped and his replacement was on standby. Every day, pressure was put on me to sign off on the staff, but I resisted taking a hasty decision in such a life-changing matter. I prayed for God's wisdom and guidance. I read the Bible more frequently than I used to and what it says of being on the side of truth and justice. I knew if I took a contrary decision, I would face unpleasant confrontation both in the short and long term and if I was in the right and followed the truth, Jesus would fight for me. Kingdoms come and pass, political parties come and go, governments come and go, but Jesus is in control forever.

Along the line, the devil was constantly reminding me of the adversaries I would face if I did not follow the directives. Some of the challenges would include losing out on my career progression, perks, favours, and the personal hatred against me by the powers in authority could be unbearable. All these could constitute a heavy baggage to start my journey in the new company. I needed to be meticulous with details and with guidance from the Lord. I called for the file of the staff, studied it meticulously and discovered that there was nothing implicating to warrant a sack. I discussed with the immediate boss of the staff who supported the sack about my findings. It was clear to him that there was nothing to justify the termination of the staff's appointment. The armour of God I needed to help me take a contrary view was, "the belt of truth, the shield of faith, and the sword of the Spirit (the Word of God)". With all these, I became bold and courageous. I stopped the sack and instead requested for management's approval to extend his employment for 6 months to enable me work with him for a while to ascertain his capability and suitability to continue with the company. My request was approved and at the end of the 6 months, his performance report was adjudged to be on the high level which led to his continuation as a permanent staff. The most interesting part of my experience was that while the sack issue was going on, hardly did I know that the staff's mother and pregnant wife were fasting and praying for

God's mercy and deliverance from the storm. My secretary released this information to me as soon as the powers that be approved the 6 months extension for the staff. Another interesting aspect was that the staff has progressed to managerial position, and at the time of concluding this book, the staff was still in the employment of the company, contributing to its success. On my part, I thank God Almighty for a successful and peaceful resolution. It was a risk worth taking and an opportunity to serve God faithfully. The first time I met the staff in person was when he came into my office to say thank you.

Initially, the fear of the unknown gripped me, but in the end, I discovered that very little was really unknown. God has made each of us unique and designed us for a purpose in life. When opportunity comes and we find that purpose, we should accept it and put our all into fulfilling it. Forget about what it costs to do what is right because ultimately we will reap a harvest of contentment. What happened was an opportunity to share my Christian faith with those around me, including those I report to, those who report to me and my colleagues. Proverbs 21:3 says, "To do what is right is more acceptable to the LORD than sacrifice".

The Word of Spirit and of Power

1 John 2:29

If you know that he is righteous, you know that everyone who does what is right has been born of him.

Hebrews 4:13

Nothing in all creation is hidden from God's sight. Everything is uncovered and laid bare before the eyes of him to whom we must give account.

1 Kings 3:9

So give your servant a discerning heart to govern your people and to distinguish between right and wrong. For who is able to govern this great people of yours?

Ephesians 6:10-12

Finally, be strong in the Lord and in his mighty power. Put on the full armour of God, so that you can take your stand against the devil's schemes. For our struggle is not against flesh and blood, but against the rulers, against the authorities, against the powers of this dark world and against the spiritual forces of evil in the heavenly realms.

Chapter 26

TRIALS

❋

The fact that we are alive means we will experience trials. Trials for example are storms of life such as disasters, mountains, emotional hurricane and specifically can be loss of livelihood, loss of employment, loss of business; pandemic, illness, unfair trial, discrimination, persecution, punishment for doing what is right, loss of loved ones and so on. These are all battles of life. Believers should fight their battles with their faith fixed on Jesus and on their knees. It is a biblical pattern. Engage God in our battles so that we are not battling alone. The battle could be a long one and you need peace and comfort as the battle goes on. We must stand firm and stay true to the one who can deliver us from anything that tries to distract us or drown us. We should always hold unto Jesus in storms of life and not let go. He says to us "Be still and know that I am God" (Ps. 46:10). Jehovah has the final say. God is eternal and a covenant keeping Father. By engaging God in our battles, we get a greater amount of peace and comfort. With God on our side, we will overcome.

In trials we should always fix our mind that whatever happens, God is in control. We are limited because we do not have the full story. Nothing happens without God's direct or indirect approval. With Jesus there is peace of mind and triumph in the day of trouble. God gets our attention when we encounter trials through restlessness which leads to constant and regular prayers. God speaks to us through circumstances. No discipline seems pleasant at the time but painful. Later on, however it produces a harvest of righteousness and peace for those who have been trained by it.

How to Prepare for Trials of Life

The time of peace is the time to prepare for the storm. When storm comes, we are already rooted and well grounded. Jesus gave us the key to surviving in the midst of trials. He wants us to build our house on the solid rock, instead of sand. The rock is Jesus. People who trust and put their faith in Jesus will survive when they face trials. Our faith and trust in Jesus is an invitation for him to come on board with us. When we put our faith and trust in him, we experience peace, comfort and assurance when we face trials. Hear and do his word and we will see His truthfulness. The Bible is not a book that we can sideline for a while. It is the word of spirit and of power. By reading and studying the Bible, God speaks to us.

Sometimes during trials what we think about abandonment is due to what God wants to perfect in our lives. Look at the blind man who was blind right from the mother's womb. He asked Jesus whether it was because of his sin or the parents. Jesus told him it was not that. It was because God wanted to glorify His name.

The story of Lazarus is also a good example of God's delay for God's purpose. Jesus loved Martha and her sister, and Lazarus. Yet when he heard that Lazarus was sick, he stayed where He was for two more days. The delay was for a purpose, to remove all doubts about raising Lazarus back to life. He said, it is for God's glory so that God's son may be glorified through it (John 11:4). God's delay in answering our prayers means it is not God's time. If you cry, it will not change God's time. He has a special time concerning your life. He will allow you go through trials but will not forget you. Stop comparing yourself to others. Even the lives of twins are different. God's purpose for your life is different. God will bring something good out of your problem but you have to be patient. You will have to persevere. God's promises never fail even though Satan wants us to believe that they will not come to pass.

With the Lord, a day is like a thousand years, and a thousand years are like a day. The Lord is not slow in keeping His promise, as some understand slowness (2 Peter 3:8-9). For my thoughts are not your thoughts neither are your ways my ways, declares the

Lord. As the Heavens are higher than the Earth, so are my ways higher than your ways and thoughts than your thoughts (Isaiah 55:8-9).

The LORD longs to be gracious to you; he rises to show you compassion, for the LORD is a God of Justice. Blessed are all who wait for him.

How to Steer Ourselves through Trials

God overcomes all obstacles. Steering ourselves through the obstacles of life, believers will need God's guidance. We have the Holy Spirit to guide us. This is not different from steering a horse, ship or plane with the help of a radar or propeller. Steering ourselves through obstacles cannot be done without God leading us. When time is tough, God will make believers shine. He will deliver us out of our troubles when we call upon him (1 Cor. 10:13, 2 Cor. 4:8-9). Be anxious for nothing but in everything give thanks to God through prayers and supplication. Be on the track of faith, trust, prayer, hope and love forever. In periods of uncertainty and trails, worry, fear, anxiety distract believers. Christ constantly encourages us to cast our cares upon him (1 Peter 5:7), and to take His yoke upon us in exchange for our burdens (Matt. 11:28-30). The name of the LORD is a strong tower; the righteous run to it and are saved (Prov. 18:10). There is peace in the midst of a storm when you put your faith in Jesus Christ.

Trials and Persecution

If you are persecuted because of your belief in Jesus, that is persecution. If you are paying a price because you are doing what Jesus says in the Bible or you are doing what is right as contained in the Bible that is persecution. But if you are paying for wrong-doing against the law of the land to satisfy your ungodly desires, you will pay for it. If you ask God for forgiveness, he will forgive you but you will still go to prison. Psalm 119:71 says, "it was good for me to be afflicted, so that I might learn your decrees".

Trials Produce Benefits

- In trials, believers share in the sufferings of Christ. His sufferings flow into our lives.
- In trials, believers experience God's comfort. We are comforted in all our troubles. What a friend we have in Jesus.
- In trials we are equipped for the ministry.
- In trials we trust in God. The God who raises the dead.
- Trials enable believers to experience insufficiency and make them call on God.
- During trials, believers experience complete inadequacy and complete reliability on God.
- In trials many will give thanks to God because He will release His favour.
- Suffering promotes character (Rom. 5:3-4).
- Suffering produces joy (1 Thess. 5:16-18).
- Suffering proves godliness (2 Tim. 3:12).

In trying times believers should be courageous and strong with complete focus on God, trusting him for solution in his own way (Josh 1:7-8). Believers should put on the armour of God to stand firm against the devil.

Waiting on God Rightly During Trials

Those who wait on God will never be disappointed, but we have to wait rightly. While waiting:

- Wait In Prayer and Praise.
- Rejoice in Hope.
- Continue to Do Good.

The Apostle Paul's example in waiting rightly for God during trials provides an excellent example for believers. Paul's letter to the Philippians was the happiest letter of Paul. In Philippians 4:4 he says, "Rejoice in the Lord always. I will say it again: Rejoice".

Paul was in prison but still he was rejoicing instead of being sad. The letter to the Philippians was supposed to be the saddest letter of Paul. But despite all his problems in Philippi, he was always rejoicing because he knew that whatever happens, God is in control. In Psalm 46:10, He says, "Be still and know that I am God".

Be joyful always; pray continually, give thanks in all circumstances, for this is God's will for you in Christ Jesus (1 Thess. 5:16-18). Pray for those who hurt you (Matt. 5:44). It is the path to victory over tribulations and persecution. Everyday make a choice to stay in faith. When faced with trials, look up and do not look around. When you look up, you will find salvation; you will find freedom; you will find mercy; you will find grace; you experience divine healing; you will find new beginning. The enemy's plans will always be turned to your advantage. The LORD longs to be gracious to you; He rises to show you compassion, for the LORD is a God of justice. Blessed are all who wait for him (Isaiah 30:18).

The Word of Spirit and of Power

Proverbs 29:25

Fear of man will prove to be a snare, but whoever trusts in the LORD is kept safe.

Psalm 23:4

Even though I walk through the valley of the shadow of death, I will fear no evil, for you are with me; your rod and your staff, they comfort me.

2 Chronicles 32:7

Be strong and courageous. Do not be afraid or discouraged because of the king of Assyria and the vast army with him, for there is a greater power with us than with him.

2 Corinthians 12:9

My grace is sufficient for you, for my power is made perfect in weakness. Therefore I will boast all the more gladly about my weakness so that Christ power may rest on me.

Psalm 27:13

I am still confident of this; I will see the goodness of the LORD in the land of the living.

Psalm 4:8

I will lie down and sleep in peace for you alone O LORD make me dwell in safety.

Romans 12:12-13

Be joyful in hope, patient in affliction, faithful in prayer. Share with God's people who are in need. Practice hospitality.

Psalm 34:19

A righteous man may have many troubles but the LORD delivers him from them all.

Isaiah 41:10

Do not fear, for I am with you; do not be dismayed for I am your God. I will strengthen you and help you; I will uphold you with my righteous right hand.

Philippians 4:6

Do not be anxious about anything, but in everything, by prayer and petition, with thanksgiving, present your request to God.

Psalm 34:15

The eyes of the LORD are on the righteous and his ears are attentive to their cry.

Isaiah 8:10

Devise your strategy, but it will be thwarted, propose your plan, but it will not stand, for God is with us.

1 John 5:14

This is the confidence we have in approaching God, that if we ask anything according to his will, he hears us.

2 Corinthians 12:10

For Christ sake, I delight in weaknesses, in insults, in hardships, in persecutions, in difficulties. For when I am weak then I am strong.

Chapter 27

GOD'S DELAY IS
NOT GOD'S TIME

When our prayers are not answered we think God has abandoned us. Sometimes what we think about abandonment is due to what God wants to perfect in our lives. He says if we pray and ask for anything according to his will, he hears us (1 John 5:14). But we must be patient in waiting and also be waiting rightly. If you cry from the mountain top, it will not change God's time. In 2 Peter 3:9 it says, "The Lord is not slow in keeping his promise, as some understand slowness. He is patient with you, not wanting anyone to perish but everyone to come to repentance". In Isaiah 55:8, the LORD declares, "For my thoughts are not your thoughts neither are your ways my ways." He has a special time for your life. God will bring something good out of your problem but you have to be patient. You will have to persevere. Be on the track of faith, hope and love forever as you wait for him.

Also bear in mind that God's delay means salvation. 2 Peter 3:15 says, "Bear in mind that our Lord's patience means salvation". Stop comparing yourself to others. Do not live the life of someone. Even the lives of twins are different. Faith based prayer and trusting God to answer our prayer in the way he knows best should be the focus (Rom. 12:12). Lord, make me what you want me to be. Ask the Lord not to give you anything you ask for if it is not what he wants for you (1 John 5:14). Ask for his will to be done in your life. Prayer is not an excuse to do nothing. Prayer should be followed with a plan of action.

The Story of Lazarus (1)

The story of Lazarus is a good example of God's delay for God's purpose. Jesus loved Martha, her sister Mary and Lazarus. Yet when he heard that Lazarus was sick, he stayed where he was for two more days. The delay was for a purpose. Jesus said, "This sickness will not end in death. No, it is for God's glory so that God's son may be glorified through it" (John 11:3-6). When Jesus finally arrived in Bethany, he found out that Lazarus had already been in the tomb for four days (John 11:17). When Mary heard about Jesus arrival, she quickly went to him and fell at his feet. When Jesus saw her weeping and the Jews who had come along with her also weeping he was deeply moved in spirit and troubled. Jesus grieved with them and wept (John 11:35-36).

The Lessons

Jesus is God. He came in human flesh and blood. What transpired is a great lesson to believers. He demonstrated to us that he is human and a man of sorrows familiar with sufferings. He shares in our sorrows and troubles. Jesus wept not because he could not raise Lazarus to life, but to demonstrate to us that he shares in our tribulations whenever we call on him. In the midst of any storm, he is in the boat with us if we invite him into the boat. He rejoices with those who rejoice and mourns with those who mourn. For whoever touches you, touches the apple of his eye (Zech. 2:8).

Why Did Jesus Delay for Two More Days?

The delay was for a purpose, which was to remove all doubts about the miracle of raising Lazarus to life. In the time of Lazarus, the Sadducees believed that the state of the dead was a place of unending sleep. They did not believe in resurrection (Acts 23:8). This meant that Lazarus could still have a chance to wake up within three days. When Jesus arrived in Bethany, Lazarus had already been in the tomb for four days (John 11:17) with no

176

chance of waking up. This was confirmed when Martha in John 11:39 said to Jesus, "By this time there is bad odour, for he has been there four days". Then in 11:40, Jesus said to her, "Did I not tell you that if you believe, you would see the glory of God". Jesus' miracles never leave any doubt afterward. The purpose of the delay was fulfilled. He silenced the enemy. Jesus' delay means it is not God's time. His ways are different from our ways (Isa. 55:8). Be patient, loving and rejoicing while waiting, because he has a purpose for everything.

God's Delay is not God's Time: My Testimony (2)

I arrived in the UK in October 1971 on a Nigerian Government scholarship to study to become a Chartered Management Accountant (CMA) at the South-West London College Centre for higher business studies. It was a full scholarship which covered my boarding and tuition fees. On arrival I moved into the South London overseas student hostel, close to South-West London College. I never changed accommodation until I concluded my studies in 1976 and returned to Nigeria in January 1977. When I received my final examination result in the summer of 1976 and saw that I passed which meant that I had completed my course of study, I gave thanks to God and pleaded for two favours:

First Request

I prayed to God to bless me and help me secure employment in the UK which would take me back to Nigeria.

Reasons for the Request

I reasoned that it was a way of paying back and saying thanks to the country that provided the funds for my education through a scholarship award. It was only fair for me to return to contribute my quota for its development. I considered that staying in the UK to work was unfair even though I already had my residence status to work in the UK.

Second Request

For the fact that I had a wonderful time in the UK after the initial settling challenges such as the weather, culture, social life, food and so on. I did settle quite quickly due to the hospitable people I met during my period of stay. Prominent among them was a Christian couple, Eyril and Audrey and their two children, Jonathan and Susan who were caring and loving. Life as I have witnessed is not made up of great sacrifices and duties but of little things in which smiles and kindness given habitually are what win and preserve the heart. In the hostel where I lived throughout my stay in the UK, I met a kind and caring warden who always joined us in the hostel chapel to worship on Sundays. In the college and outside the college, I met really good people. All these experiences left a great impression on me and I developed a great likeness for the UK. Based on these I requested God to bless me with the opportunity to return to the UK with a good employment to payback to a country where I got my higher education and to reunite with the good people I and my wife Grace met, especially Eyril and Audrey.

How Did God Grant these Requests?

First Request

Prayer is not an excuse to do nothing. Prayer has an action plan. Although there was no job vacancy advertisement for accountants at UAC International, fortunately I saw an advert in one of the daily newspapers where UAC International Blackfriars Road SE1 advertised for vacancies for engineers. I was moved to put in an application for the position of an accountant in the month of September 1976. Frankly I never expected a reply from the company. But surprisingly on the 5 October 1976, I received a letter from the Personnel Department inviting me for an interview at 10:30am on 14 October 1976 at UAC House, Blackfriars Road SE1. I attended the interview and on 29 October 1976, I received a second letter inviting me for a final interview at 2pm on Thursday, 9 November 1976. The letter also stated that a medical examination was also arranged for me at 3pm on the same day. Finally on 11 November 1976, I received a letter offering me the position of an accountant in their Nigerian subsidiary headquarters, UAC of Nigeria Lagos, Nigeria. God granted my request and even gave me more than what I requested for, Hallelujah. UAC of Nigeria was the largest conglomerate and most successful company at the time. What I never expected in life, he made it possible for me. I returned to Nigeria with the best job. I returned on 28 January 1977 and I commenced work on 1 February 1977. It took less than three months for the first part of my prayer to be answered.

Second Request

The second request as I have stated earlier was like a dream and looked impossible. While in Nigeria, to secure good employment which will return me back to the UK to payback to a country where I got my higher education, enjoyed much love and hospitality was unthinkable. My thinking was not different from that of my wife. To us it looked like a dream but still we never gave up in praying for the will of God to be done. We had the trust that with him, nothing is impossible. On the 30th of September 1980, I saw an advertisement in the Daily Times of Nigeria where Nigerian National Petroleum Corporation (NNPC) was inviting applications for the position of Accountants. I thought about it for a few days and prayed then decided to apply for the vacant positions. Within two weeks I was invited for an interview. After a couple of weeks I was offered employment. This necessitated my leaving UAC of Nigeria to NNPC to begin a new career in June 1981. In Psalm 46:10 he says, "Be still and know that I am God". I was still confident in hope that the change was for the better and would not affect God's plan for my life. Since my early working life, I cultivated the habit of arriving at work quite early and stayed beyond the quitting time. I continued with the same attitude when I joined the NNPC. The early arrival to work leaves me with some extra minutes before the starting time which I used for glancing through a few headline news in the dailies. Deacon

D.C. Obi, a colleague and a friend also came to work early and joined me to glance through the dailies before returning to his office. One morning in late September 1984, he came with an OPEC job vacancy advert dated 17th September 1984 which he showed me and asked whether I was interested. I took it from him and glanced through it. I noticed that it was a wonderful opportunity. I photocopied it and returned his copy. He told me that he was equally interested. Both of us applied. I routed my application through the official channels (my boss, personnel and OPEC Governor for Nigeria).

At this time nothing was certain because of the fierce competition from other OPEC member countries. I waited for quite a while to hear from OPEC headquarters in Vienna, Austria. Thank God finally I was invited for an interview on 29 May 1985, after 8 months waiting. I travelled to Vienna and I was interviewed. On 15 August 1985, I received a letter of offer of employment to commence work on or before November 1985. I resumed work at the OPEC headquarters in Vienna, Austria on October 1985. I am still thankful to God because at that time in Nigeria, living was very difficult as a result of the foreign debt burden, indigenisation policy, and the dreaded structural adjustment programme (SAP) which inflicted untold hardship on citizens. For me and my family, the foreign job window was an escape route provided by the God Almighty. It was a rescue mission by the Almighty God to safety and plenty, coming at the most critical time. Later, I tried to make some meaning out of the OPEC employment. I thought God had blessed me with it in replacement or exchange for my original request I made to him in 1976, which was for good employment that would take me back to the UK. My wife, Grace and I were very grateful to God for the OPEC job because such opportunities do not come easily. However, we continued to hope in prayers for God's will to be done.

The waiting continued until my OPEC employment contract ended in 1993 after eight years. My hope started wavering. My contract in OPEC was to end in October 1993. OPEC officers are always given extra six months to take care of disruptions caused by children schooling programme. It had never been refused. The decision to extend was usually taken by the OPEC board of governors six months to the departure of the officer. To comply with that provision, the secretary general applied for my extension for six months starting in October 1993 after the expiration of my contract. The extension application was made to the board of governors' meeting in April 1993. Surprisingly the governors did not approve my extension for school year citing budget constraint as reason for non-approval, despite my commendable services to the organization. However little did I know that what was playing out was in fulfillment of God's plan for me. When the news first got to me about the rejection of my extension application by the board, my wife and I were thrown off balance. We felt very bad. Later we picked ourselves up. There is nothing that happens that God does not directly or indirectly permit. We gave thanks to God for the opportunity we have had. We started making the necessary arrangements for returning back to Nigeria in October 1993. As was usually done, I had to write to NNPC management in Lagos, giving them advance notice of the end of my OPEC contract without school year extension. In the notification I informed them that I would return to NNPC in October 1993 and adequate arrangement should be made to take care of my resettlement. While waiting for NNPC's reply to my letter, I received a fast mail from NNPC Lagos. When the mail was opened, I and my wife were shocked that it was a letter informing me that I have been posted to NNPC's London office. The letter was dated 13 July 1993. My assignment in London was to head the NLNG Escrow Secretariat for managing the NLNG shareholders' funds.

At the end my wife and I realized that the school extension saga was an act of God. He used it to stop me from getting the six months extension because the London job was waiting by the corner. More also if I had got the school year extension I would have been denied the London job. God answered my two prayer requests made in 1976. The first request was answered in 1976 in less than 3 months while the second prayer request was answered in 1993 after 17 years. Later I also realised that God took 17 years to prepare me for the London assignment which was quite challenging.

My dream to return back to Nigeria with good employment to join in the development of the country was realized. So also my dream to return to the UK with good employment and to payback for the love and hospitality I and my wife received was realized.

Many Things to Thank God for Answered Prayer Requests I Made In 1976

I served and contributed to the Nigerian economy both locally and internationally. I was able to give back to the UK by way of giving employment to UK citizens, payment of income tax, and NHS contributions. I am also very grateful to God that a project which could not take off for 20 years before I joined the company succeeded. My assignment in the UK was concluded at the end of 1997. God turned six months denied to five years. I returned in 1998 with a promotion to the position of General Manager Finance, Nigeria LNG Limited. Furthermore, the head office of Nigeria LNG Ltd, a company I served and gave my best through the help of the Almighty God is located in my community Amadi-Ama. Finally, I got the opportunity to know God better, share my Christian faith both in Nigeria and with the wider world. Hallelujah. What an amazing grace. God's delay in answering prayers is not an abandonment as revealed by my testimony. For every true believer God's promises are yes, in Christ (2 Cor. 1:20).

God has a purpose for everyone. God's delay in answering prayers is for a purpose. We are limited because we do not have the full story. We only know what humans can know. If you believe and have faith in God, you will trust him to answer your faithful prayers in the way he knows best. How Christ sees you is of more importance than how others do or even how you see yourself. Christ sees your potential and destiny and knows what you can become when you put your implicit trust in him.

The Word of Spirit and of Power

Hebrews 6:15

After waiting patiently, Abraham received what was promised.

1 John 5:14-15

This is the confidence we have in approaching God; that if we ask anything according to His will, He hears us. And if we know that He hears us, whatever we ask, we know that we have what we asked of him.

Psalm 37:4-5

Delight yourself in the Lord and he will give you the desires of your heart. Commit your way to the LORD; trust in him.

Romans 12:12

Be joyful in hope, patient in affliction, faithful in prayer.

2 Peter 3:8

But do not forget this one thing, dear friends: with the Lord a day is like a thousand years, and a thousand years are like a day.

Isaiah 55:8-9

For my thoughts are not your thoughts, neither are your ways my ways, declares the LORD. As the heavens are higher than the earth, so are my ways higher than your ways and my thoughts than your thoughts.

Isaiah 30:18

The LORD longs to be gracious to you; he rises to show you compassion, for the LORD is a God of justice. Blessed are those who wait for him.

James 1:17

Every good and perfect gift is from above, coming down from the Father of the heavenly lights, who does not change like shifting shadows.

Psalm 113:7-8

He raises the poor from the dust and lifts the needy from the ash heap; He seats them with princes.

Psalm 116:1-2

I love the Lord, for he heard my voice; he heard my cry for mercy. Because he turned his ear to me, I will call on him as long as I live.

Chapter 28

STEWARDSHIP OF TIME

Stewardship of time is biblical. Although God is outside the constraints of time (Ps. 90:2; 2 Pet. 3:8), humanity is constrained by time. The Bible states the specific number of years humans can live on Earth. Believers are also humans and are constrained by time. Time is the sequential ordering of events, having a beginning and an end. Because everyone has to account for one's stewardship on Earth thus stewardship of time becomes very necessary for believers. Time plan will make believers bear more fruit within their lifetime. The Bible has an account of God's plan for his creation, with a beginning and an end. God's time plan has a beginning starting with creation, ending with judgment and new creation with the locus around the life, death and resurrection of Jesus Christ (Mark 1:15). God has also specifically established definite times for the end and final judgment (Luke 21:31). However the timing of the end is only known to the Father (Matt. 24:36; Mark 13:32). A time plan is a key driver in the stewardship of time. The Christian journey requires a road map and a time plan. It helps believers not only in navigating the journey but also in finishing.

Church Activities

Stewardship of time must take cognisance of church activities. Churches have plans for growing in the word of God and sharing the word of God. Churches publish yearly church calendars, diaries and books with lectionary. Weekly church activates are also displayed or published by churches to guide their members and others in their daily spiritual walk. Believers should have their daily plans that accommodate these activities. However although church activities are necessary for promoting the work of the ministry, they should not be allowed to get in the way of fulfilling the calling of believers which is putting God first in their lives. God needs believers both in the church and outside the church. Sometimes our religious lives can become an impediment in fulfilling the purposes of God in our lives. It is outside the church we can become instrument of peace. It is outside the church we can show mercy or dispense justice or show love. These are the things that bring glory to God. In Matthew 9:13, Jesus' answer to the Pharisees, shows that the merciful life of believers should precede their religious life. The parable of the Good Samaritan (Luke 10:25-37) is also clear on this point. The true neighbour is the one who shows love, mercy and kindness in affliction. Sometimes we are overwhelmed with church activities and other aspects of our calling outside the church such as loving, showing mercy, kindness, dispensing justice, forgiveness and so on are ignored or minimised. The priest and the Levi never cared for the afflicted. They did not see beyond their religious activities. The Samaritan, who is a pagan, cared. He showed mercy, love and kindness. In Luke 10:37 Jesus says, "Go and do likewise".

Honour God with Your Time

Jesus sacrificed his life to save us from sin and to make us justified before God. To honour God with our time is part of the sacrifice believers must make. Find time to seek opportunities to serve and witness. Plan an inclusive time. God is a jealous God. He demands our loyalty and wants first place in our lives. These facts must be factored into the stewardship of believer's time. Hobbies, recreation, holidays and so on are good but should not be allowed to take the first place and put God in secondary position in our lives. The same thing applies to important things such as family, church activities, career, and country. They should be managed in a way so that they do not get in the way of placing God first in our lives.

Time for Your Employers

Work (career) for daily living should be adequately accommodated in your daily activity plan but should be done in a way not to get in the way of giving complete loyalty to God and placing him in first position in your life. The workplace provides opportunity to demonstrate Christ's nature in us by loving, showing mercy, justice, patient, kindness and so on. Daily time plans should also make provision for doing likewise outside work environment. During the work hours, give your best to your employer. It is Biblical and is one of the best investments you can make. The parable of the talents (Matt. 25:14-30) is clear on service to an employer. Obey them not only to win their favour when their eye is on you, but like slaves of Christ, doing the will of God from your heart. Serve wholeheartedly as if you were serving the Lord not them (Eph. 6:6-7). Work is service to God (Col. 3:17, 22-24). Work is important for human dignity as well as survival. Idleness is condemned (Prov. 10:4; 12:24; 2 Thess. 3:10-15).

Work is a good gift from God. Do not use your employer's work hours to read the Bible, hold prayer meetings, hold fellowship meetings or carry out activities that are not part of your work. Such practices will affect your output. They are in conflict with what the Bible says. Give to Caesar what belongs to Caesar. The lunch time and tea break are your personal free time which you can use to read your Bible or do other things. What counts at work is your personal example to others. Let people see Jesus' nature through your lifestyle. If you live a godly life at work, you will be a shining example of what Jesus stands for. Your example should bring thanksgiving to God. With your lifestyle you can save souls for Jesus.

Time for the Family

Have time for the family in your daily activity time plan. People in the Bible were family centered. Families form the foundation of society. Members of families should spend time together to honour God. Read the Bible together, share the word together, share experiences and testimonies and sing praises to God. A godly and loving atmosphere in your home is the foundation for your life. If you have God, you will always have company and love. It is the process of building godly family values. A peaceful society is built on godly family values. It is a service to God and humanity. Finally, what you sow is what you reap (Gal. 6:7). In selecting officers for appointment in the church, family background is one of the qualities that is considered (1 Tim.3:4; Titus 1:6). Having said these, family activities must not be allowed to put God in a secondary position, in our lives. God must always come first. The family must be seen to be involved in neighbourly love. They must show love, mercy, kindness, justice and so on to others.

Recreation and Others

Recreation, hobbies and others are good but God must come first. It may seem a hassle to take time to exercise but in the long run, it will save you time due to the fitness and wellness that come with it. It disciplines the mind and exerts the body with exhaustive physical activity. Some basic exercise involves cycling, walking, running, swimming etc. Exercise is Biblical. The Bible says that physical training is of some value (1 Tim 4:8). Healthy living might give you more time to live and serve God.

Time is Unpredictable

Believers need to bear in mind that decisions of yesterday could be seriously challenged by present circumstances. Commitment to the Lord Jesus Christ must be kept alive day by day and every moment. Covid-19 has taught us that the world is unpredictable and nothing is certain. We should always live our life with the end in mind. Forget about yesterday. It is gone forever. Tomorrow is not yet yours. Today is what you own. Make the best use of it. Decide today to serve Jesus rightly by walking every moment with him. Godliness has value for all things, holding promise for both the present life and the life to come (1 Tim. 4:8). Apply your time and resources wisely. Stewardship of time is therefore very central in a believer's life. Jesus did not reveal the date or time of his second coming but expects us to be ready to receive him when he comes (Luke 12:35-40). We are expected to be prepared always by living a godly life. In walking faithfully, we need to be time conscious. Christ expects that believers should be good stewards of their time and material resources, because at the end, all will give account of their lives on earth. More than half of your life will be spent at the workplace or marketplace and other engagements of life. In every area of life you find yourself, remember that you are the messenger. Your life should speak for Jesus.

Chapter 29

STEWARDSHIP OF MATERIAL RESOURCES

— ❊ —

Jesus expects believers to use their material resources (the gifts and opportunities) he has given them to serve him faithfully and not to use them to please men (Gal. 1:10). The focus is faithfulness in the way we use the material resources God has blessed us with. Wise living makes believers to handle worldly wealth for the kingdom purpose.

Wealth and Riches

God is not against wealth and riches. Christians should see these gifts and opportunities as blessings and favours from God. Proverbs 10:22 says, "The blessing of the Lord brings wealth and he adds no trouble to it". Wealth and honour come from God (1 Chron. 29:12). Everything we have accomplished comes from God (Isa. 26:12). Every good and perfect gift is from above, coming down from the Father of the heavenly lights (James 1:17). A man can only receive what is given him from Heaven. Psalm 112:1-3, tells us that "Wealth and riches are in the house of persons who fear the LORD". "Fear the LORD" is not in the sense of terror but in the sense of deep respect, deep honour, deep reverence and deep love by putting him first in all we do. King Solomon's wealth was seen as a favour from God. God told King Solomon, "I will give you what you have not asked for, both riches and honour, so that in your lifetime you will have no equal among kings" (1 Kings 3:13). Abraham's attitude towards wealth and riches is a model for believers to follow. He acknowledged God as his sole source of wealth when he rejected the gifts (plunder) from the king of Sodom. Abraham said to the king of Sodom, "I have raised my hand to the LORD, God Most High, creator of Heaven and Earth, and have taken an oath that I will accept nothing belonging to you, not even a thread of the thong of a sandal, so that you will never be able to say I made Abraham rich" (Gen. 14:22). Isaiah 26:12 says, "LORD you establish peace for us; all that we have accomplished you have done for us".

Warning about Riches

Christians must be mindful of how they come about their wealth and riches because not all wealth and riches come from God or have his approval. Wealth and riches acquired through dishonest means, greed, corruption, bribery, unjust means and so on do not have God's approval.

What the Bible Says About Such Wealth and Riches:

Watch out. Be on your guard against all kinds of greed; a man's life does not consist in the abundance of his possessions (Luke12:15). Dishonest money dwindles away, but he who gathers money little by little makes it grow (Prov. 13:11). Like a partridge that hatches eggs it did not lay, is the man who gains riches by unjust means. When his life is half gone they will desert him, and in the end, he will prove to be a fool (Jer. 17:11). Keep your lives free from the love of money and be content with what you have because God has said "Never will I leave you; never will I forsake you" (Heb. 13:5). Do not trust in extortion or take pride in stolen goods; though your riches increase do not set your heart on them (Ps. 62:10). People who want to get rich fall into temptation and a trap and into many foolish and harmful desires that plunge men into ruin and destruction. For the love of money is a root of all kinds of evil. Some people, eager for money, have wandered from the faith and pierced themselves with many grieves (1 Tim. 6:9-10). Again I tell you, it is easier for a camel to go through the eye of a needle than for a rich man to enter the kingdom of Heaven (Matt. 19:24). Therefore I tell you, do not worry about your life, what you will eat or drink; or about your body, what you will wear. Is not life more important than food and the body more important than clothes? Who of you by worrying can add a single hour to his life? (Matt. 6:25; 27). Give us each day our daily bread (Luke 11:3). Keep your lives free from the love of money and be content with what you have, because God has said, "Never will I leave you; never will I forsake you" (Heb. 13:5).

The Love of Money and Riches:
The Glamour and Reality

To start with, God is not against wealth and riches but we should be aware of the fact that not all wealth and riches come from God or have his approval. The Bible is the word of God and the authoritative guide for all believers. The word of God is the absolute truth and what it says is the absolute truth for our spiritual growth and conduct. The Bible condemns the love of money and riches. It says in 1Timothy 6:9-10, "People who want to get rich fall into temptation and a trap and into many foolish and harmful desires that plunge men into ruin and destruction. For the love of money is a root of all kinds of evil. Some people, eager for money, have wandered from the faith and pierced themselves with many griefs".

From my experience, the love of money cannot make us conduct ourselves in a manner worthy of the gospel of Christ. Anyone who puts money and materialism first before God, will not have the ability to serve God. God is a jealous God and he does not want any competition for our loyalty to him (Nah. 1:2). Money changes people and not for good. The dark side of money can be explained as follows: The love of money can influence behaviours that we are unaware of. Money can spark unlawful behaviours such as stealing, cheating, bribery, extortion, forgery and other forms of corruption and negative behaviours. The love of money can affect ethics and moral judgment. The love of money does not understand wrong and right. The love of money does not understand the language of mercy, kindness, compassion, sharing, forgiveness, contentment,

192

goodness, self-control, selflessness and so on. Self-interest takes precedence over anything else.

Furthermore, there is the insatiable want for more. The more money they have, the more money they want. The love of money leads to addiction such as drug, and food. The love of money leads to materialism. Wealthy people want to have everything and can buy anything they want at any time. Couples who love money and strive for wealth and material possessions are more likely to head towards divorce. Materialism is linked to lower satisfaction in a relationship. Studies have proved that children who grow up in wealthy families have a higher risk for psychological disorders such as depression, eating disorder or anxiety. Children who are born rich also are more likely to become addicted to drugs, food, gambling, alcohol, and materialism such passion for and unlimited appetite for designer clothes, custom made cars and so on.

Although there is hardly anything more desired in the world than money, but the reality of money is often far different from the glamour. Wealth is linked with addiction to drugs, alcohol, gambling and many ungodly practices. Wealth leads to such practices as social inequality and segregation. People are killed because of money, relationships breakdown because of money, trillions are lost in gambling all over the world because of wanting to make more money. Money cannot buy love or happiness. The love of money and material possessions can prevent us from making the teaching about God our saviour attractive. Truly the love of money cannot make us conduct ourselves in a manner worthy of the gospel of Christ.

I will conclude this very important topic with three quotations from the Bible. The first is what Jesus said to his disciples about riches in Mathew 19:23-24, then Jesus said to his disciples, "I tell you the truth, it is hard for a rich man to enter the kingdom of heaven. Again I tell you, it is easier for a camel to go through the eye of a needle than for a rich man to enter the kingdom of God". Then secondly what Apostle Paul said in his letter in Hebrews 13:5, Keep your lives free from the love of money and be content with what you have because God has said, "Never will I leave you; Never will I forsake you". Then thirdly, Apostle Paul's letter to Timothy: 1 Tim. 6:17-19, "Command those who are rich in this present world not to be arrogant nor put their hope in wealth, which is uncertain, but to put their hope in God, who richly provides us with everything for our enjoyment. Command them to do good, to be rich in good deeds, and to be generous and willing to share. In this way, they will lay up treasure for themselves as a foundation for the coming age, so that they may take hold of the life that is truly life". Finally, although wealth and riches may not have kingdom value but their proper use has kingdom consequences (1 Tim. 6:19).

The Word of Spirit and of Power

Proverbs 27:24

For riches do not endure forever, and a crown is not secure for all generations.

Psalm 39:6

Man is a mere phantom as he goes to and fro: He bustles about, but only in vain; he heaps up wealth, not knowing who will get it.

Mathew 6:19-21

Do not store up for yourselves treasures on earth, where moth and rust destroy, and where thieves break in and steal. But store up for yourselves treasures in heaven, where moth and rust do not destroy, and where thieves do not break in and steal. For where your treasure is, there your heart will be also.

Hebrews 13:5-6

Keep your lives from the love of money and be content with what you have, because God has said, "Never will I leave you; Never will I forsake you, so we say with confidence, "The Lord is my helper; I will not be afraid".

Luke 12:15

Then he said to them, "Watch out. Be on your guard against all kinds of greed; a man's life does not consist in the abundance of his possessions".

Mathew 6:25, 27

Therefore I tell you, do not worry about your life, what you will eat or drink; or about your body, what you will wear. Is not life more important than food, and the body more important than clothes? Who of you by worrying can add a single hour to his life?

Mathew 6:24

No one can serve two masters. Either he will hate the one and love the other, or he will be devoted to the one and despise the other. You cannot serve both God and money.

Showing Godly Attitude towards Wealth and Riches

Christians must avoid having an arrogant attitude towards wealth and riches by failing to acknowledge God as the source of wealth (Deut. 8:17-18). Wealth and riches should be viewed according to God's centered perspective. God is the one who provides our daily needs and he wants us to trust him for our provisions (Matt. 6:25, 27). God is the owner of all things and we are only stewards and administrators of God's wealth and riches. We need not forget that a time will come when we will give account to God for the use of our wealth (1 Cor. 10:31).

Jesus says we should seek the kingdom of God first rather than his material blessings and these things will be given to us as well. Proverbs 22:1 says, "A good name is more desirable than great riches; to be esteemed is better than silver or gold". Favouritism of the rich over the poor is condemned as sin (James 2:1-4).

Giving

Giving is a decision that comes from love. You cannot love without giving. Giving brings joy to us and others. Giving is a planned lifestyle. Be wise in giving. What a man sows is what he will reap (Gal. 6:7). Giving to the needy areas of society is one of the objectives of a focused ministry. This is one of the areas Christianity can impact society and bring change.

Jesus in Matthew 25:40 has given believers a list of people to help. He called them "the least of these" which includes those that no one else will care for them. Remembering the words Jesus himself said, "it is more blessed to give than to receive".

Generosity

Believers should be loving, for love comes from God. Anyone who loves has been born of God and knows God. With sufficient love in our heart, we will give out of poverty. No one is so poor that he has nothing to share. Also no one is so rich that he has nothing to need from someone else. Believers should live a life of generosity. You cannot talk of God's generosity without also being generous with the little you have. Hebrews 13:16, 6:10, tells believers not to forget to do good and to share with others, for with such sacrifices God is pleased. God is not unjust: He will not forget your work and the love you have shown him as you have helped his people and continue to help them.

Wealth and riches come with the duty to give generously to those in need (Prov. 11:24). Believers should learn from the example of Jesus, "though he was rich, yet for our sake he became poor, so that we through his poverty might become rich" (2 Cor. 8:9). Thus material offerings to Christ should not be a burden (1 Cor. 9:11). Sacrificial giving is also an expression of love to the Lord (2 Cor. 9:12) and brings thanksgiving to God from those who received it (2 Cor. 9:11). Wealth and riches themselves do not have eternal value, however their proper use has eternal consequences (1 Tim. 6:19).

Jesus Wants Us to Give Wisely

He said we should be careful not to do our acts of righteousness before men to be seen by them. If you do, you will have no reward from your Father in Heaven (Matt. 6:1). Your giving should not be done for human approval. Do not do good deeds to be admired by people. Love your enemies, do good to those who hate you (Luke 6:27).

Do Not Store Up Earthly Treasures

Believers are asked not to store up earthly treasures. Earthly treasures can be stolen, lost or ruined. Jesus said believers should not store up earthly treasures; because where their treasures are, that is where their heart will be. Believers should instead store up treasures in Heaven by doing good, because Heaven is where moth and rust do not destroy and thieves do not break in and steal (Matt. 6:19-21).

Be Good Stewards of Material Resources

Believers should avoid the mentality of insatiable lust for worldly passions and desires. The mentality of insatiable lust for material resources are outside the teaching of Christ. Believers should spend their material resources on things that will honour God such as giving to the Ministry, the needy, charity and even to enemies that are in need.

Giving to the Ministry

Believers should use their material resources to promote the work of the ministry (support churches, evangelism, missions). The most important harvest in giving to the ministry is the salvation of souls. If you give to the ministry you will be sowing the word (Mark 4:14) and you will be reaping from it. Freely you give, freely you will reap. Giving to the needy areas of society is a support to focused ministry.

Offering and Tithing

Believers should support the ministry through their offering and tithing. Malachi warns against slackness in tithing (Mal. 3:8-10). Amos uses ironic expression to show that tithing cannot replace righteousness (Amos 4:4).

Likewise Jesus condemns the scribes and Pharisees for neglecting justice, mercy and faithfulness while tithing

197

meticulously. Instead they should practice all of these (Matt. 23:23).

In Luke 11:42, Jesus said, "Woe to you Pharisees, because you gave God a tenth of your mint, rue and all other kinds of garden herbs, but you neglect justice and the love of God. You should have practiced the latter without leaving the former undone".

Hebrews identifies three types of sacrifices that believers should offer: praise, good deeds and sharing with those in need (Heb. 13:15-16).

Believers cannot replace righteousness with gifts, offerings, tithes and donations. These practices without also practicing righteousness, love, justice, mercy and faithfulness are condemned by our Lord Jesus. Believers should watch out that acts of offerings and gifts are not done as the Pharisees did. They did for human approval with no reward from Heaven. Grow above human praise.

Offering and Sacrifice

In the biblical usage, offering and sacrifice are interchangeable. Offering refers to a gift of devotion and more of a general nature. In the Old Testament, "Sacrifice" refers to peace offering. Sacrifices were offered to God to honour God and thank him for his goodness. Sacrifices enabled God's people to be made right with God by atoning for their sins. God's wrath against sin and sinners is just as much as a New Testament consideration as an Old Testament one. God still considers those who are sinful and unrighteous to be his "enemies" (Rom. 5:10, Col. 1:21). Jesus ended the Old Testament type of sacrifice. He is the sacrificial lamb. He paid for our sins through his death on the cross.

The end of the Old Testament type of sacrifice does not mean that those who come to God through Jesus Christ no longer bring sacrifices. But instead of animals and grain offerings, spiritual sacrifices are required (1 Peter 2:15). Believers should emulate the saviour, Jesus Christ by offering themselves as a living sacrifice devoted to God (Rom. 12:1). Everything believers do in this life to honour God such as walking in righteousness, faithfulness, humility, love, truthfulness, forgiveness, justice, etc. becomes an offering acceptable to God (Rom. 15:16); even to the extent of martyrdom which is considered as a drink offering (Phil. 2:17).

The Word of Spirit and of Power

Romans 12:13

Share with God's people who are in need. Practice hospitality.

Mathew 6:1, 3

Be careful not to do your "acts of righteousness" before men, to be seen by them. If you do, you will have no reward from your Father in heaven. When you give to the needy, do not let your left hand know what your right hand is doing.

Mathew 5:16

In the same way, let your light shine before men that they may see your good deeds and praise your Father in heaven.

Mathew 25:40

"I tell you the truth, whatever you did for one of the least of these brothers of mine, you did for me".

1 Corinthians 3:8

The man who plants and the man who waters have one purpose, and each will be remembered according to his own labour.

2 Corinthians 8:12

For if the willingness is there, the gift is acceptable according to what one has, not according to what he does not have.

2 Corinthians 9:6-7

Whoever sows sparingly will also reap sparingly and whoever sows generously will also reap generously. Each man should give what he has decided in his heart to give not reluctantly or under compulsion, for God loves a cheerful giver.

Mark 9:41

I tell you the truth; anyone who gives you a cup of water in my name because you belong to Christ will certainly not lose his reward.

Proverbs 11:25

A generous man will prosper; he who refreshes others will himself be refreshed.

Hebrews 6:10

God is not unjust; he will not forget your work and the love you have shown him as you have helped his people and continue to help them.

Chapter 30

STEWARDSHIP OF THE ENVIRONMENT: CARING RESPONSIBILITY AND SHOWING NEIGHBOURLY LOVE

---------------- ✻ ----------------

The environment is part of God's creation and demands the attention of believers. In the biblical times, humans were ignorant about climate change (global warming). God created a world that is very good (Gen. 1:31) and put humans that he made in his own image to rule over it (Gen. 1:27-28). The Bible is God breathed and has many facts that can support environmental awareness in the present world. God intended the humans he made in his image to 'work and take care' of the garden that he has given them (Gen. 2:15). God did not permit harm to be done to the environment in pursuit of our social and economic goals. In Genesis 8:21-22 and Psalm 65:9-13, God says he will never curse the ground or destroy any living creatures. He waters the ground for crops and plants to grow so that we can reap bounty harvests. In Deuteronomy 11:11-15, Israel has a duty to care for the land he has given them. Certain limitations in the use of the land and its crops are to be observed.

God commanded the Israelites to care for the land that he has given them. In Deuteronomy 11:11-12 God says, "But the land you are crossing the Jordan to take possession of is a land of mountains and valleys that drinks rains from Heaven. It is a land the LORD your God cares for; the eyes of the LORD your God are continually on it from the beginning of the year to its end". Likewise believers have caring responsibility for the environment because humans are made in God's image and are God's representatives on earth to care for his creation. Humans are made to help God in his ruling of his creation. They represent God in the creation. The caring of God's creation is what shows God's image in humans (Gen 1:26-31, 2:15-17). The environment is part of God's creation. Creation is not evil, although it has been corrupted as a result of human sin. God loves the world he has made. We should do likewise. He created the world and blessed it and says it is very good (Gen 1:31).

"Dominion and Subdue"

"Dominion and subdue" are caring responsibilities. They are commands from God to rule his creation and take care of it. God created an orderly world from emptiness and disorder (Gen 1:2) and intended mankind he made in his image to "work and take care" of the garden that he has given them (Gen 2:15). In Genesis 1:28, "Dominion and Subdue" do not give permission to excessive exploitation. We are tasked by God to be caretakers of creation. The environment is part of God's creation. Christians have the caring responsibility. Humans are entitled to pursue social and economic progress but should be done in harmony with nature (environment).

Environmental Challenges

The environment consists of land, mountains, valleys, sky, water, air, forests, oceans, rivers, plants and all living creatures in them. The challenges the environment is faced with include: extinction, deforestation, overexploitation, humanity's excessive intrusion and infringement into nature, vast illegal wildlife trade, pollution caused by uncontrolled emissions into the air, waste discharges into water bodies and land etc. God did not permit harm to be done to the environment in pursuit of our social and economic progress.

Benefits of the Environment

- The mysteries, aesthetic, and recreational values of the environment bring thanksgiving, reverence, honour and praise to God.

- Provides us with food.
- Provides us with quality air.
- The environment sustains life and the natural balance of our planet.
- The aesthetic value of the environment has a calming effect on humans.
- It can be looked at as something of beauty for mere enjoyment to restore the spirit and perspective of man.
- It increases and enriches human experience in the quest for recreation and relaxation.

What Does the Bible Say About Caring for the Environment?

Genesis 1:27-28 (KJV)

"So God created man in his own image, in the image of God create he him; male and female created he them. And God blessed them, and God said unto them, be fruitful and multiply, and replenish the earth and subdue it; and have dominion over the fish of the sea and over the fowl of the air, and over every living thing that moveth upon the earth".

Genesis 1:29-30

Then God said, "I give you every seed bearing plant on the face of the whole earth and every tree that has fruit with seed in it. They will be yours for food. And to all the beasts of the Earth and all the birds of the air and all the creatures that move on the ground – everything that has the breath of life in it – I give every green plant for food". And it was so.

Genesis 2:15

The LORD God took the man and put him in the Garden of Eden to work it and take care of it.

How can Christians Contribute to Caring for the Environment?

Everyone has the ability to impact positively on environmental protection by getting involved in such noble activities as supporting climate change mitigation and adaptation, involvement in plant gardens, tree planting, and supporting conservation clubs or setting up conservation clubs in schools, supporting environmental charities, NGO's and so on.

I am a Chartered Accountant and by studying the Bible, I became interested in contributing my little bit in protecting the environment. I started with reading environmental books and journals published by the accounting institutes and others. I have also participated in environmental seminars and workshops which included a training workshop on Clean Development Mechanism which was organised in collaboration with the Foreign and Commonwealth Office of the United Kingdom. From these sources I became aware of the type of contributions I could make. I have organized seminars jointly with the Ministry of environment on environmental protection in Nigeria. I have also written a book titled *Balancing Commercial Interests with Environmental and Socio-economic Responsibilities in the Nigerian Oil and Gas industry.* I have also contributed a paper to the government titled *Institutional reforms necessary to make the various sectors of the economy climate change compliant.* Mankind is expected to be compatible with nature. We must not abuse it, but we must use it. It is God commanded.

The fact still remains that if the environment continues to suffer human neglect, the present and future generations will suffer greatly. Due to global warming caused by unsustainable human activities, the natural world is presently experiencing extreme weather such as extreme heat, devastating storms and drought. The threat to human health is alarming. In addition to caring responsibility for God's creation by humans, neighbourly love should be a motivation for Christians to support environmental protection. Love your neighbour is much bigger than what we think. In the Old Testament, 'Neighbourly Love' which is love your neighbour as yourself was restricted to people we know, those around us, those who belong to the same group, such as those who looked the same or spoke the same language and so on (Levi 19:18). In the New Testament, Jesus from the lessons of the Good Samaritan shows us that neighbourly love is far wider than that (Luke 10:25-37). From the parable of the Good Samaritan, Jesus expanded neighbourly love to include everyone who needs our mercy and compassion. We should follow examples of the Good Samaritan which demonstrated Kingdom Neighbourliness. In Luke 10:37 Jesus says, "Go and do likewise". Philippians 2:3 says, "Do nothing out of selfish ambition or vain conceit but in humility consider others better than yourselves". Unsustainable environmental practices adversely affect biodiversities and affect their capacities to perform their functions and sometimes lead to extinction of some species. Adverse environmental challenges will affect future generations.

How Was the Environment Created: What Does the Bible Say?

Genesis 1:11-12

Then God said "let the land produce vegetation; seed-bearing plants, and trees on the land that bear fruit with seed in it, according to their various kinds". The land produced vegetation; plants bearing seed according to their kinds and trees bearing fruit with seed in it according to their kinds. And God saw that it was good.

Genesis 1:6-8

And God said, 'Let there be an expanse between the waters to separate water from water". So God made the expanse and separated the water above it. God called the expanse "Sky".

Genesis 1:9-10

And God said, "Let the water under the sky be gathered to one place and let dry ground appear". God called the dry ground "Land" and the gathered waters he called "Seas". And God saw that it was good.

Genesis 1: 20-22

And God said "Let the water teem with living creatures, and let birds fly above the earth across the expanse of the sky." So God created the great creatures of the sea and every living and moving thing with which the water teems according to their kinds, and every winged bird according to its kind. And God saw that it was good. God blessed them and said "Be fruitful and increase in number and fill the water in the seas, and let the birds increase on earth."

Genesis 1:24-25

And God said, "Let the land produce living creatures according to their kinds; livestock, creatures that move along the ground and wild animals, each according to its kind". God made the wild animals according to their kinds, the livestock according to their kinds, and all the creatures that move along the ground according to their kinds. And God saw that it was good.

Exodus 23:10-11

For six years you are to sow your fields and harvest the crops, but during the seventh year let the land lie unploughed and unused.

Leviticus 19:23-25

When you enter the land and plant any kind of fruit tree, regard its fruit as forbidden. For three years you are to consider it forbidden, it must not be eaten. In the fourth year all its fruit will be holy, an offering of praise to the LORD. But in the fifth year you may eat its fruit. In this way your harvest will be increased. I am the LORD your God.

Leviticus 25:2-5

Speak to the Israelites and say to them, "When you enter the land I am going to give you, the land itself must observe a sabbath to the LORD. For six years sow your fields, and for six years prune your vineyards and gather their crops. But in the seventh year the land is to have a sabbath of rest, a sabbath to the LORD. Do not reap what grows of itself or harvest the grapes of your untended vines. The land is to have a year of rest.

Mathew 22:37-39

Jesus replied, "Love the Lord your God with all your heart and with all your soul and with all your mind". This is the first and greatest commandment. And the second is like it: "love your neighbour as yourself".

Philippians 2:3

Do nothing out of selfish ambition or vain conceit but in humility consider others better than yourselves.

Deuteronomy 11:11-12

But the land you are crossing the Jordan to take possession of is a land of mountains and valleys that drinks rain from heaven. It is a land the LORD your God cares for; the eyes of the LORD your God are continually on it from the beginning of the year to its end.

The Environment Brings Thanksgiving and Praise to God

Ecotourism is driven by the desire to experience the natural environment (nature) and the world such as wildlife, wilderness, jungle, wetland, biodiversities, rivers, coastlines, lakes, mountains, valleys, and so on. These sceneries provide lasting beauty and recreation opportunities. They are looked at as something of lasting beauty for mere enjoyment to restore the spirit and perspective of mankind. Their aesthetic qualities bring reverence, praise and honour to the creator our God.

Example:

One of the most popular Christian praise and worship hymns 'How Great Thou Art' that made a huge impact on unevangelised places and the unsaved from the early 1930s was written out of the love for the environment in appreciation and thanksgiving to God for His awesomeness in creation. 'How Great Thou Art' is a favourite hymn of praise with God's people, and gospel singers going back to its history. This popular inspirational Christian worship hymn is also commended by Evangelist Billy Graham when he said "The reason I like "How Great Thou Art" is because it glorifies God. It turns Christians' eyes toward God, rather than themselves. I use it as often as possible because it is such a God honouring song." The original Swedish text was a poem titled 'O store Gud' written by a Swedish pastor Carl Boberg, in 1886. He was one of the leading evangelical preachers of his day. His inspiration for this text is said to have come from a visit to a beautiful country estate on the southeast coast of Sweden. He was suddenly caught in a midday thunderstorm with formidable moments of flashing violence, followed by a brilliant sun. Soon afterwards, he heard the calm, sweet songs of the birds in nearby trees. The experience prompted him to fall to his knees in humble adoration of his Mighty God.

The history of the hymn shows that the Boberg's version was translated into the German language by Manfred Von Glehn, under the title of 'Wie gross bist Du'. In 1925 Rev. Gustav Johnson of North Park college, Chicago, Illinois made the first literal English translation from the Swedish text which is titled, 'O Mighty God, When I Behold The Wonder'. S Prokhanoff translated the German version into Russian language, in 1912. Rev SK Hine and his wife Mercy, English missionaries, while ministering in Ukraine in 1933 learned the Russian translation of 'O store Gud'. They were astonished that the hymn had a striking effect in unevangelised places on the unsaved. Amid unforgettable experiences which Rev SK Hine and his wife had in the Carpathian Mountains, came with the thoughts of the first three verses in English were born. The mountain scenery played a central role in writing the original English lyrics to this hymn. When the World War broke out in 1939, Rev Hine and his wife returned to Britain where he continued his gospel campaigns. The fourth verse of the hymn was not written until after the war.

The hymn was introduced to American audiences in 1951 when Mr James Caldwell sang 'How Great Thou Art' at Stony Brook Bible Conference on Long Island. Cliff Barrows and Rev Shea of the Billy Graham Evangelistic Team used it during the famed London Crusade in Harringay Arena.

Verse 1 and 2 of 'How Great Thou Art'

1. O Lord my God, when I in awesome wonder,
Consider All, the Worlds thy hands have made,
I see the stars, I hear the rolling thunder,
Thy pow'r throughout, the universe displayed.

Chorus:
Then sings my soul, My Saviour God to thee,
How Great Thou art, How Great Thou art,
Then sings my soul, My Saviour God to thee,
How Great Thou art, How Great Thou art.

2. When through thy woods and forest glades I wonder,
And hear the birds sing sweetly in the trees,
When I look down, from lofty mountains grandeur,
And hear the brook and feel the gentle breeze.

What Does the Bible Say?

Songs of songs 2:11-13

See! The winter is past; the rains are over and gone. Flowers appear on the Earth; the season of singing has come, the cooing of doves is heard in our land. The fig tree forms its early fruit; the blossoming vines spread their fragrance. Arise, come my darling; my beautiful one, come with me.

Chapter 31

DAD'S HARVEST GIFT BROUGHT SADNESS

❈

I was not born into a wealthy family as I mentioned earlier. Dad and my grandparents brought me up because I lost my mother when I was a toddler. My dad was a subsistence fisherman. He cast net and we lived out of his daily catches which we sold to buy food daily. He was very loving and hardworking, always making sure that we lived each day in full. I was growing up in the era of superstitious beliefs, juju worship, idol worship, native doctors, secret societies, ghost stories and so on. The good news was that my dad completely abstained from these practices. He advised me always that these practices were evil and that Jesus is against such practices. Even when he fell ill, he never allowed any native doctor to attend to him. He totally relied on medicines from hospitals and pharmacies.

His commitment to the Lord shaped my life. Sadly, as I was growing up, I never saw him go to church to worship on Sundays. He would dress me up and lead me to the church and later come to collect me. Fortunately, he will never stop talking to me about Jesus. I was a bit jealous because the fathers of some of my friends stayed with them to worship together. Many a times I would ask him "Nna," (dad) "why do you not want to worship with me in the church?" My dad was an introvert. He guards what comes out of his mouth. He will only tell me "Do not worry; God is with you in the church". This went on for some time but later I started becoming anxious. My friends started asking why my father never attended the church. The meaning then was that, if you did not attend church on Sundays, then you are not a Christian. I decided to summon courage to confront my father. He so loved me that he never wanted to hear me cry or weep before him.

On one of the Sundays, I cried and wept bitterly before him asking him to attend the church worship and stay with me to the end. He could not help it. He was forced to tell me the whole truth.

His Story

He told me that as I have seen and witnessed his mother (my grandmother) was a very committed Christian. She never missed worship services. Even when she was sick she made it to the church believing that Jesus would cure her. So that was how he was brought up. He was a committed church elder. He went on. He said to me that in his days, the harvest thanksgiving offerings and gifts were very competitive among the villagers. During one of the harvest seasons, he promised that he would give Jesus the best gift. Quite early enough he started preparing and saving up some cash from his daily catches. When he had saved enough for the harvest, he decided to buy a rare and highly valued gift at that time. During my father's time, the tinned corn beef was expensive and highly valued. He decided to buy a tin of corn beef for the harvest to thank Jesus. My father being one of the church elders, he usually joined in preparing the church for the Sunday worship. The Saturday leading to the harvest Sunday he joined in the decoration of the church. As always was the case, all the harvest gifts were used in decorating the church. Most of these gifts included varieties of gifts such as smoked fishes, yams, plantains and so on and my dad's corn beef, which was unique.

He said the purpose of decorating and displaying the gifts in the church was to honour God and thank him for the harvest and ask for more blessings. He said because the village church was small it was not run by a pastor but by an agent. Since the village had no pastor to conduct the harvest worship service, as usual a pastor from Okrika district church was sent. He arrived on Saturday evening in preparation for the harvest service on Sunday. My dad was full of hope and joy that Jesus would accept his unique gift and bless him. He said on the Sunday morning, he dressed up in his new harvest traditional dress. When he arrived at the church he noticed other gifts but his tinned corn beef was missing. He said he was shocked to the bones. He started making enquiries of the whereabouts of his tinned corn beef gift. He met one of the church workers and he was told that the pastor was taking his breakfast with his tinned corn beef. He said he wanted to confirm it himself. He was taken to the pastor's abode where he met him enjoying a plate of rice with his tinned corn beef meant for the harvest. He said the pastor never waited for his gift to go through the usual harvest processes when thanksgiving prayers are offered in return for God's blessings before he consumed it. That was the end of his church attendance. He was no longer a church goer on Sundays. His harvest joy turned into sadness.

He continued to believe and trust in Jesus. To make up for the lost ground, he usually invited the Jehovah witness preachers to preach the Bible to him but he did not belong to their body. I was a little boy and did not know much about the Bible. Because I was about 8 years old, I did not have a good grasp of the Bible; I could not change his thinking and help him overcome the trauma. He always believed he gave all he had to Jesus but the pastor stopped his blessings. But I know very well that my father received his reward no matter what happened. God is not limited. He is a personal God. He knows everything about individuals.

My dad's name is Alfred. He passed on to be with the Lord when I was in class 4 in the grammar school. I am convinced that God blessed his harvest gift which overflowed to me and my children. It is through Jesus' righteousness that we are made righteous. It is not by gifts or by works so that no one can boast. Dad's unforgiveness was out of ignorance and limited knowledge about God. Pastors are our spiritual leaders. In my father's generation, pastors were regarded as representatives of God on Earth. I would believe the pastor gave thanks for the corned beef and the plate of rice before he took his breakfast. That would have made up for the harvest thanksgiving. Apostle Paul in Ephesians 4:26-27 says, "In your anger do not sin. Do not let the sun go down while you are still angry". If I knew the Bible as I do today,

I would have read this passage to him. In Luke 17:1, Jesus said to his disciples "Things that cause people to sin are bound to come, but woe to the person through whom they come". These are appropriate Bible passages for the actions of my father and the pastor and other believers who may encounter such challenges.

Chapter 32

WORDS OF WISDOM

- *God is good not because you do good but because he is good.*
- *The biproduct of knowing Christ and doing what he says is peace.*
- *Under the new agreement Jesus has already done the work. In the old agreement, you have to do the work.*
- *If you chose not to forgive, you are trapped in your past. To forgive is to experience freedom.*
- *Grace is the unmerited favour of God.*
- *If you boast of your righteousness, it is based on your faith in Jesus but not on your own righteousness.*
- *When time is tough God will make believers shine.*
- *How do we know the truth? Study the Bible and you will know the truth.*
- *There are not many ways to God but only one way which is Jesus.*
- *Faith under fire produces total victory.*
- *God did not promise smooth sailing, but he promises smooth landing.*
- *Praise him with the same intensity when your prayers are not answered.*
- *It is not what you believe that makes you a Christian but what you obey. Nicodemus believed in Jesus but did not obey him.*
- *God does not hold our sins against us, but Satan does. We are dead to sin does not mean that we are incapable of committing sin. To sin or not to sin depends on your old nature and your new nature.*

- *Sin cannot hold dominion over us for we are not under the law but under grace.*
- *Grace does not give us authority to condole sin.*
- *God did not save us from sin and wants us to still stay in sin.*
- *Prayer life is where your life is set around prayers.*
- *Prayer is God's appointed way to get what you need.*
- *Prayer helps us to get things which money cannot buy – healing, wisdom, journey mercies, security etc.*
- *Nothing that we face is a surprise to God. Find strength through adversity.*
- *Distance does not affect the love of Jesus, because God is a personal God.*
- *Fear activates the devil, just as faith activates God.*
- *If you spend time with fearful people, you will adopt fear. Fear breeds fear.*
- *Don't live somebody's life with somebody else's expectations.*
- *If you love God, your ending will be better than your beginning.*
- *If you love God, you will have the ability to love others.*
- *If you love God, you must keep his commandments.*
- *Going to church does not mean that you love God, because the devil also goes to church.*
- *The church will not change you, unless you are hearing something and understanding and doing it.*
- *The new covenant is the offer of friendship with Christ.*
- *Prayer does not mean doing nothing. Prayer has an action plan.*
- *To serve is a manifestation of Christianity. Jesus served.*
- *I can trust God with what is next. He did it before, he can do it again.*
- *Salvation cannot be by church membership. Baptism is a testimony of salvation.*
- *Walking in love is walking in victory. Living in love is living in victory.*
- *Excited and jumping for Christ is good but it is not only how high you can jump for Christ but also doing what he says*
- *Be careful about what you hear and how it affects your belief.*

- *Evaluate what you hear. Make sure it is in line with what you believe.*
- *We have to do what we hear. We have to apply what we hear. Be doers of the word and not just hearers.*
- *We hear the word; we receive it and do it.*
- *Be faithful when nothing is changing. He sees you doing the right thing when things are not working.*
- *There is no limit to God's favour. There is no limit to God's blessings.*
- *One man's obedience made us righteous.*
- *Faith without action is dead but also action without faith is dead.*
- *Righteousness and justice are the foundation of God's throne.*
- *Resurrection is a proof that he has cleared us from our sins.*
- *The world operates on the basis of fear. Christians operate on the basis of faith.*
- *Fear and danger are not the same. Danger is very real. Fear is a choice – David and Goliath.*
- *Fear is a product of things you create in your mind. The only thing we have to fear is fear itself.*
- *The law is righteous but cannot give you forgiveness or grace. You have to fulfill what it says.*
- *The law was given through Moses. But Jesus brought grace.*
- *If you are led by the spirit, you are not under the law.*
- *Do not say I am committed as long as it is going well. Do not give up on what you have set to achieve. Be stubborn when it comes to quitting.*
- *Stay committed to your job no matter whether your supervisor likes you or not. Commitment outlasts difficulty. God is saying stay committed.*
- *In Christ a man and woman are made one. In Christ black and white are made one. In Christ husband and wife are made one.*
- *If you are led by the spirit, you are not under the law. You can never go wrong following the spirit.*
- *Sweat is a curse of human effort.*

- *Lord forgive me, I will not do it again is the talk of the flesh but confessing your sins before the Lord in a humble manner is spirit led.*
- *Jesus is my righteousness. On my own I am not righteous. That I am born again is not righteousness. Christ is my righteousness.*
- *When you start with self-righteousness and obeying the law, then you are falling from grace.*
- *Abel was murdered by his brother Cain. The blood of Abel was crying for revenge. The blood of Jesus was singing for forgiveness, voice of grace.*
- *In difficult times we do not look around but look up. Be strong and very courageous. Tough times do not last but tough people do.*
- *Belief is a matter of the heart. Out of your heart proceeds the issues of life, actions of life. If you really believe in your heart it will really proceed to action.*
- *The Bible is a book that you cannot sideline for a while.*
- *The Bible is one of the greatest resources Christians have but it has been under-utilised.*
- *God does want everyone to be saved and not to perish. But it is left to the individual's decision to accept to be saved.*
- *You must confess your sins and forsake the sins.*
- *Derive your security from the Lord. Say Lord, I give you my security. Remove false security from me.*
- *Faith is incomplete without corresponding action.*
- *In the Old Testament you have to keep the 10 commandments before you are saved but in the New Testament it is not so. Christ has already made the sacrifice.*
- *Repentance is a daily experience.*
- *Live life with simplicity by living one day at a time. Give us today our daily bread.*
- *Focus on today and let it count. Live life in full today. Jesus will meet all your needs. He never fails.*
- *Jesus talks about sacrificial love. Love that put other people before us. Love one another as I have loved you.*
- *Selfless love is you first, not me first.*

- *Genuine love demands self-denial. Love sacrificially.*
- *Our LORD's patience means salvation.*
- *In every area of life you find yourself, remember you are the messenger. Your life should speak for Jesus.*

CPSIA information can be obtained
at www.ICGtesting.com
Printed in the USA
LVHW111911260922
729328LV00002B/10